꽉! 잡은 중학 영문법

1
Book

GRAMMAR
CATCH

KB037671

Happy House

How to Use This Book

주요 문법 설명

내신 성적 향상을 위한 필수 영문법을 체계적으로 설명해 줍니다. 여러분이 보다 쉽게 이해할 수 있도록 학교 시험에 자주 출제되는 예문들을 담았습니다.

Grammar Check-Up

'내신 족집게 문제'를 풀기 위한 워밍업 단계로, 각 단원의 주요 문법에 관한 다양한 문제 풀이를 통해 기초 실력을 확인할 수 있습니다. 우리말 해석 및 영작 문제를 풀며 독해와 작문 실력을 향상시키며, Word Tip을 통해 문제 해결 능력을 키울 수 있습니다.

내신 족집게 문제

각 단원의 문법 사항 중에서 학교 시험에 자주 출제되는 주요 문법 문제들을 엄선하여 주관식과 객관식 문제로 구성했습니다. 문법 문제를 보다 쉽게 풀 수 있는 노하우를 알려드립니다.

수능 감각 기르기

사고력과 분석력을 키워 주는 문제들을 통해 중학교 영문법에 자신감을
갖게 됩니다. 앞서 학습한 단계의 문제들을 기반으로 수능 문제에 대한
감각을 키울 수 있도록 구성했습니다.

서술형 즐기기

그림이나 표를 이용한 서술형 문제를 다양하게 접할 수 있습니다.
앞서 학습한 Grammar Check-Up의 영작 문제에서 확장된
'한 단락 영작 학습'을 통해 Writing 실력을 향상시킬 수 있습니다.

Workbook

본책에서 학습한 내용을 복습하고 각 Unit 별로
더욱 다양한 유형의 문제들을 풀어 보면서 배운 문법을
완벽히 마스터할 수 있도록 도와줍니다.

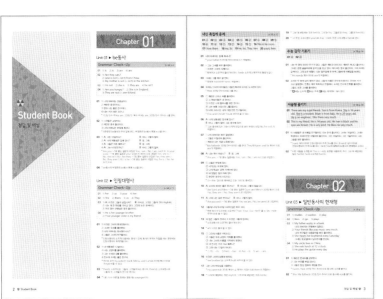

정답 및 해설

본책 및 워크북에서 여러분이 푼 문제들에 대한 정답과 저자의
명쾌한 설명이 담겨 있습니다. 문제를 풀면서 미처 생각하지
못하고 넘어간 부분을 확인하고, 틀린 문제는 다시 한 번 풀어 보세요.

Contents

Chapter 01

be동사와 인칭대명사
- ✿ Unit 01 be동사
- ✿ Unit 02 인칭대명사

Chapter 미리보기

	인칭	주어	현재형	줄임말	부정문	의문문
단수	1인칭	I	am	I'm	I am not	Am I ~?
	2인칭	You	are	You're	You are not	Are you ~?
	3인칭	He She It	is	He's She's It's	He is not She is not It is not	Is he ~? Is she ~? Is it ~?
복수	1인칭	We	are	We're	We are not	Are we ~?
	1인칭	You		You're	You are not	Are you ~?
	3인칭	They		They're	They are not	Are they ~?

It's a piece of cake. 그것은 케이크 한 조각이다.
▶ 누워서 떡 먹기

01 be동사

A | be동사

be동사의 현재형은 am, are, is이며, 주어에 따라 다르게 사용된다. '~이다, ~있다'라고 해석한다.

	인칭	주어	be동사의 현재형	줄임말
단수	1인칭	I	am	I'm
	2인칭	You	are	You're
	3인칭	He/She/It	is	He's/She's/It's
복수	1인칭	We	are	We're
	2인칭	You		You're
	3인칭	They		They're

ex • I am (= I'm) 14 years old.
  • He is (= He's) in the living room.

B | be동사의 부정문

be동사 뒤에 not을 쓴다. '~이 아니다'라고 해석한다.

Tips
• am not은
  줄여 쓸 수 없다.

긍정문	부정문	줄임말
I am	I am not	I'm not
He is She is It is	He is not She is not It is not	He's not = He isn't She's not = She isn't It's not = It isn't
We are You are They are	We are not You are not They are not	We're not = We aren't You're not = You aren't They're not = They aren't

ex She is very tall. → She is not very tall.

C | be동사의 의문문

be동사를 주어 앞에 놓는다. '~입니까?'라고 해석한다.

긍정문	의문문	긍정 대답	부정 대답
I am	Am I ~?	Yes, you are.	No, you aren't.
You are	Are you ~?	Yes, I am.	No, I'm not.
He is She is It is	Is he ~? Is she ~? Is it ~?	Yes, he is. Yes, she is. Yes, it is.	No, he isn't. No, she isn't. No, it isn't.
We are You are They are	Are we ~? Are you ~? Are they ~?	Yes, you/we are. Yes, we are. Yes, they are.	No, you/we aren't. No, we aren't. No, they aren't.

ex A: Is John handsome? B: Yes, he is. / No, he isn't.

Grammar Check-Up

Note

O1 빈칸에 알맞은 be동사의 현재형을 쓰시오.

1) My father _____ a teacher.

2) Karen _____ Chinese.

3) Ann and I _____ good friends.

4) You _____ very tall.

2) Chinese 중국인

O2 다음 문장을 지시대로 바꾸어 쓰시오.

1) They're cats.

의문문 ▶ _____

2) Jane is from China.

부정문 ▶ _____

3) My mother is in the kitchen.

부정문 ▶ _____

O3 다음 질문에 대한 대답을 완성하시오.

1) Ⓐ Are you 10 years old?　　Ⓑ No, _____.

2) Ⓐ Is your sister at home?　　Ⓑ Yes, _____.

3) Ⓐ Are they very pretty?　　Ⓑ Yes, _____.

4) Ⓐ Is he your friend?　　Ⓑ No, _____.

O4 다음 우리말을 영작하시오.

1) 너 배고프니?

→ _____

2) 그녀는 영국에 있다.

→ _____

3) 그들은 친절하지 않다.

→ _____

1) hungry 배고픈

2) England 영국

Unit 02 인칭대명사

인칭대명사란 사람이나 사물을 가리키는 말이다. 1인칭은 나, 2인칭은 너, 너희들, 3인칭은 그, 그녀, 그것, 그들을 지칭한다.

	인칭	주격	소유격	목적격	소유대명사
단수	1인칭	I (나는)	my (나의)	me (나를)	mine (나의 것)
	2인칭	you (너는)	your (너의)	you (너를)	yours (너의 것)
	3인칭	he (그는) she (그녀는) it (그것은)	his (그의) her (그녀의) its (그것의)	him (그를) her (그녀를) it (그것을)	his (그의 것) hers (그녀의 것) —
복수	1인칭	we (우리는)	our (우리의)	us (우리를)	ours (우리의 것)
	2인칭	you (너희들은)	your (너희들의)	you (너희들을)	yours (너희들의 것)
	3인칭	they (그들은)	their (그들의)	them (그들을)	theirs (그들의 것)

Tips
- you and I = we
- he and I = we
- you and she = you
- he and she = they

A 주격

문장에서 주어 역할을 하며, '~은, ~는, ~이, ~가'로 해석한다.

ex • These are my friends. They are good tennis players.
그들은

B 소유격

소유를 나타내며, '~의'로 해석한다.

ex • It is your car.
너의

• That is her cell phone.
그녀의

C 목적격

동사의 목적어 역할을 하며, '~을, ~를, ~에게'로 해석한다.

ex • I love you.
너를

• He likes her.
그녀를

D 소유대명사

소유된 것을 나타내며, '~의 것'으로 해석한다.

ex • This is my book. = This book is mine.
나의 것

• That is our house. = That house is ours.
우리의 것

Grammar Check-Up

정답 및 해설 p.2

Note

O1 다음 중 알맞은 것을 고르시오.

1) This is   her | hers   cell phone.

2) She likes   us | our .

3) Is   your | you   mother an office worker?

4) They are   she | her   friends.

1) cell phone 휴대전화
3) office worker 회사원

O2 밑줄 친 부분을 알맞은 인칭대명사로 바꾸시오.

1) My sister is 12 years old.   (→ _____)

2) I like cats.   (→ _____)

3) He likes Sumi and me.   (→ _____)

4) Minsu and Sumi are good friends.   (→ _____)

O3 밑줄 친 부분에 주의하여 다음 문장을 우리말로 해석하시오.

1) Ⓐ Is this their ball?   Ⓑ No, it is not theirs.

→ _____

2) I have a dog. Its eyes are gray.

→ _____

3) Our English teacher is from England.

→ _____

2) gray 회색

O4 다음 우리말을 영작하시오.

1) 그는 그녀의 남동생이다.

→ _____

2) 너의 여동생은 나의 친구이다.

→ _____

O1 빈칸에 들어갈 알맞은 것을 고르시오.

_____ your father at home?

① Are ② Is ③ Am
④ Do ⑤ Does

O2 빈칸에 공통으로 들어갈 알맞은 것을 고르시오.

• He likes _____ very much.
• This is _____ watch.

① me ② her ③ their
④ us ⑤ you

O3 빈칸에 들어갈 알맞은 것을 고르시오.

She knows _____ very well.

① my ② their ③ him
④ our ⑤ yours

O4 빈칸에 들어갈 수 없는 것을 고르시오.

_____ are in the library.

① We ② He ③ Her children
④ They ⑤ Mary and Sumi

O5 밑줄 친 부분을 괄호 안의 인칭대명사로 바꿀 때 알맞지 않은 것을 고르시오.

① Karen likes Mr. Smith. (→ him)
② The monkeys are mine. (→ They)
③ This is for my grandmother. (→ her)
④ He usually helps Chris and me. (→ us)
⑤ You and Chris are my best friends. (→ They)

O6 대화의 빈칸에 들어갈 알맞은 것을 고르시오.

A: Is your brother in England?
B: _____. He is in China.

① Yes, he is ② No, he isn't
③ Yes, I am ④ No, I am not
⑤ Yes, he isn't

O7 빈칸에 들어갈 be동사를 순서대로 바르게 짝지은 것을 고르시오.

• My father _____ very handsome.
• They _____ from Italy.
• Karen and I _____ in New York now.

① is – are – am ② am – are – is
③ is – are – are ④ are – are – am
⑤ is – are – is

O8 대화의 빈칸에 들어갈 알맞은 것을 고르시오.

A: Are you thirsty?
B: Yes, _____.

① I don't ② I am ③ I am not
④ I do ⑤ you are

O9 밑줄 친 부분의 의미가 나머지와 다른 것을 고르시오.

① They are in the kitchen.
② Chicago is in America.
③ My school is near the park.
④ My socks are under the bed.
⑤ London is the capital of the United Kingdom.

[10-11] 대화의 빈칸에 들어갈 알맞은 것을 고르시오.

10
> A: Are Sumi and Mimi good friends?
> B: No, _____.

① she is   ② she isn't
③ they are   ④ they aren't
⑤ he isn't

11
> A: Are you and I in the same class?
> B: No, _____.

① I am   ② I am not
③ we are   ④ we aren't
⑤ they aren't

12 빈칸에 들어갈 수 <u>없는</u> 것을 고르시오.

> _____ house is very big.

① He   ② Their   ③ Your
④ Our   ⑤ Her

13 빈칸에 알맞은 단어를 순서대로 바르게 짝지은 것을 고르시오.

> This house is _____.
> = This is _____ house.

① him – his   ② theirs – their
③ mine – me   ④ their – theirs
⑤ her – hers

14 다음 중 줄임말이 <u>잘못</u> 연결된 것을 고르시오.

① is not = isn't   ② are not = aren't
③ am not = amn't   ④ he is = he's
⑤ you are = you're

15 다음 중 올바른 문장을 고르시오.

① It's name is Kitty.
② They like our cat Kitty.
③ I don't remember hers name.
④ Are your friend tall and pretty?
⑤ He and I am not 12 years old.

[16-17] 밑줄 친 부분을 알맞은 인칭대명사로 바꾸어 문장을 다시 쓰시오.

16 This is <u>her brother's</u> room.

→ _____

17 I love <u>my parents</u>.

→ _____

[18-20] 우리말과 일치하도록 빈칸에 알맞은 말을 쓰시오.

18
> 이것은 나의 개이다. 그것의 이름은 블랙키이다.
> → This is _____ dog. _____ name is Blacky.

19
> 그는 그의 부모님을 사랑한다. 그들도 또한 그를 사랑한다.
> → _____ loves _____ parents.
> _____ love _____, too.

20
> 이 모자는 네 것이고, 저 모자는 그녀의 것이다.
> → This hat is _____ and that hat is _____.

정답 및 해설 **p.3**

01 다음 글의 밑줄 친 부분 중 어법상 **틀린** 것을 고르시오.

> I have two foreign friends. ① They are Karen and Mike. Karen is from Canada. ② She has curly black hair and brown eyes. Mike is from England. ③ His hair is brown. His eyes ④ is blue. I email ⑤ them once a week.

- foreign 외국의 ■ curly 곱슬머리의
- once a week 일주일에 한 번

01 다음 표를 보고 빈칸에 들어갈 알맞은 말을 쓰시오.

Name	Nationality	Age	Job
Sue	Korea	16	student
Brian	Italy	20	engineer

These are my e-pal friends. Sue is from Korea.
_____ is 16 years old. _____ _____
a student. Brian is from Italy. He _____
_____ _____ old. _____ _____
an engineer. I like them very much.

02 다음 빈칸에 들어갈 말로 가장 적절한 것을 고르시오.

Somi has two brothers. Ⓐ_____ names are Minsu and Minho. Minsu is tall and handsome. Minho is very clever and kind. Somi likes Minsu and Minho. Ⓑ_____ like Ⓒ_____, too.

	Ⓐ		Ⓑ		Ⓒ
①	They	–	They	–	she
②	They	–	Their	–	her
③	Their	–	They	–	her
④	Their	–	Their	–	she
⑤	Them	–	They	–	her

02 다음 우리말을 읽고 바르게 영작하시오.

이 사람은 내 친구이다. 그는 14살이다.
그의 머리는 검은색이고, 그의 눈은 갈색이다.
그는 매우 친절하다. 그는 나를 매우 좋아한다.

_____

_____

_____

_____

Chapter 02

일반동사

Chapter 미리보기

	현재형	현재진행형
형태	동사원형 또는 동사원형-(e)s	am/are/is + 동사원형-ing
의미	현재의 상태나 반복적 동작 표현 (~하다)	현재 하고 있는 동작 표현 (~하고 있다)
부정문	주어 + do/does + not + 동사원형	am/are/is + not + 동사원형-ing
의문문	Do/Does + 주어 + 동사원형 ~?	Am/Are/Is + 주어 + 동사원형-ing ~?

Haste makes waste. 서두름이 낭비를 만든다.
▶ 서두르면 일을 그르친다.

Unit 03 일반동사의 현재형

A 일반동사

be동사(ex am, are, is, was, were)와 조동사(ex will, can, may)를 제외한 동작이나 상태를 나타내는 동사(ex play, live, like, have, study, eat, watch)를 말한다.

Tips
- 1인칭 → I, we
- 2인칭 → you
- 3인칭 → he, she, it, my father 등(I, we, you를 제외한 모든 명사 및 대명사)

주어		일반동사의 형태
1인칭 단수	I	study hard. play. get up early. have a cat.
2인칭 단·복수	You	
모든 복수	We They Sumi and Karen	
3인칭 단수	He She Your friend Karen It	studies hard. plays. gets up early. has a cat. works.

ex
- My sister and I walk to school.
- Timmy does his homework.
- My friend eats pizza for lunch.
- The dog plays with the ball.
- He and she go to the bookstore on Sunday.

B 주어가 3인칭 단수일 때 동사에 -s 붙이는 법

ⓐ 대부분의 동사는 동사원형에 -s를 붙인다.	like → likes
ⓑ -s, -ch, -sh, -o, -x로 끝나는 동사는 -es를 붙인다.	pass → passes catch → catches wash → washes go → goes fix → fixes
ⓒ 〈자음 + -y〉로 끝나는 동사는 y를 i로 고치고 -es를 붙인다. 〈모음 + -y〉로 끝나는 동사는 -s를 붙인다.	try → tries play → plays
ⓓ 불규칙 동사	have → has

ex
- He likes Italian food.
- She washes her face with cold water.
- Michael tries to do his best.
- My sister plays badminton after school.
- She has a scarf around her neck.

Grammar Check-Up

정답 및 해설 p.3

O1 다음 중 알맞은 것을 고르시오.

1) Karen study ǀ studies Korean.

2) He wash ǀ washes his hair every day.

3) They play ǀ plays computer games all the time.

3) all the time
항상

O2 우리말과 일치하도록 빈칸에 알맞은 말을 쓰시오.

1) 그녀는 꽃을 매우 좋아한다.

→ She _____ flowers very much.

2) 우리는 일요일마다 교회에 간다.

→ We _____ to church on Sundays.

3) 나의 아버지는 토요일마다 테니스를 치신다.

→ My father _____ tennis on Saturdays.

2) on Sundays
= every Sunday
일요일마다

O3 다음 문장의 일반동사에 밑줄을 긋고 우리말로 해석하시오.

1) My father works in a bank.

→ _____

2) Your friends like pop music very much.

→ _____

3) She meets her boyfriend every Saturday.

→ _____

1) bank 은행
2) pop music 대중음악

O4 다음 우리말을 영작하시오.

1) 나의 삼촌은 중국에 산다.

→ _____

2) 그녀는 12시에 점심을 먹는다.

→ _____

3) 그는 매일 기타를 친다.

→ _____

3) play the guitar
기타를 치다

일반동사의 부정문과 의문문

A 일반동사의 부정문

주어가 3인칭 단수일 때는 does not (= doesn't)을 동사원형 앞에 쓰고, 그 외의 주어일 때는
do not(= don't)을 동사원형 앞에 쓴다.

Tips
• don't/doesn't 뒤에는
항상 동사원형을 쓴다.

	주어	do 동사의 형태	일반동사의 형태
1인칭 단수	I	do not (= don't)	play. get up early. have a cat.
2인칭 단·복수	You		
모든 복수	We They		
3인칭 단수	He She Your friend	does not (= doesn't)	play. get up early. have a cat.
	It		work.

B 일반동사의 의문문

do나 does를 문장 맨 앞에 쓴다.

	do 동사의 형태	주어	일반동사의 형태
1인칭 단수 2인칭 단·복수 모든 복수	Do	I you we they	play? get up early? have a cat?
3인칭 단수	Does	he she your friend	play? get up early? have a cat?
		it	work?

C 대답하기

ex • A: Do you have a cat? B: Yes, I do. / No, I don't.
• A: Do they get up early? B: Yes, they do. / No, they don't.
• A: Does he work hard? B: Yes, he does. / No, he doesn't.

━⊕ do/does는 일반동사와 조동사로 모두 쓰인다. 일반동사일 때는 '~하다'로 해석되고, 조동사일 때는
일반동사의 부정문과 의문문을 만들 때 사용된다.
ex • I do my best. (일반동사) • I do not like her. (조동사)

Grammar Check-Up

O1 다음 중 알맞은 것을 고르시오.

1) Do | Does your father drive a car?

2) They don't | doesn't go to bed late.

3) Does he live | lives in Chicago?

4) My sister doesn't like | likes dolls very much.

O2 다음 문장을 지시대로 바꾸어 쓰시오.

1) She reads a book every day.

의문문 ▶ _____

2) They play soccer after school.

의문문 ▶ _____

3) He has an MP3 player.

부정문 ▶ _____

O3 다음 질문에 대한 대답을 완성하시오.

1) Ⓐ Does she like ice cream?

Ⓑ No, _____.

2) Ⓐ Does your father teach math?

Ⓑ Yes, _____.

3) Ⓐ Do you go to school by bus?

Ⓑ No, _____.

O4 다음 우리말을 영작하시오.

1) 너는 내 이름을 알고 있니?

→ _____

2) 수미는 아침에 우유를 마시지 않는다.

→ _____

A 현재진행형의 형태와 의미

〈be동사(am, are, is) + 동사원형-ing〉의 형태로 사용되며, '~하고 있다, ~하는 중이다'로 해석한다.

ex • It is raining now. (지금 비가 오고 있다.)
• They are playing soccer at the moment. (그들은 지금 축구를 하는 중이다.)

─⊕ 상태를 나타내는 동사 (ex have, see, hear, love, like)는 진행형을 쓰지 않는다.

ex • She has many books. (○)
• She is having many books. (×)
• She is having lunch. (○) (단, 동작을 의미할 경우 진행형 가능)

Tips
• 현재의 반복적인 동작이나 습관을 나타낼 때는 현재형을 쓴다.

B 현재진행형의 부정문

be동사의 현재형(am, are, is) 뒤에 부정어 not을 붙이며, '~하고 있지 않다'로 해석한다.

am/are/is + not + 동사원형-ing

ex • He is not (= isn't) wearing a watch.

C 현재진행형의 의문문

be동사의 현재형(am, are, is)을 주어 앞에 놓는다.

Am/Are/Is + 주어 + 동사원형-ing ~?

ex • A: Is he playing the piano?   B: Yes, he is. / No, he isn't.
• A: Are you doing your homework?   B: Yes, I am. / No, I'm not.

D 미래시제 대용

현재진행형은 soon, tomorrow, tonight 등의 단어와 함께 쓰여 가까운 미래를 나타낸다.

ex • The train is leaving soon. (기차가 곧 떠날 것이다.)

E 동사원형에 -ing 붙이는 법

ⓐ 대부분의 동사는 동사원형에 -ing를 붙인다.	learn → learning
ⓑ -e로 끝나는 동사는 e를 빼고 -ing를 붙인다.	come → coming
ⓒ -ie로 끝나는 동사는 ie를 y로 고치고 -ing를 붙인다.	die → dying
ⓓ 〈단모음 + 단자음〉으로 끝나는 동사는 끝자음을 한 번 더 쓴 후 -ing를 붙인다.	sit → sitting

Grammar Check-Up

정답 및 해설 p.4

Note

01 다음 문장을 지시대로 바꾸어 쓰시오.

1) She waits for him.

현재진행형 _____

2) He watches TV.

현재진행형 의문문 _____

1) wait for ~을 기다리다

02 다음 중 알맞은 것을 고르시오.

1) Are you doing | do your homework?

2) Is | Are | Do | Does your father driving a car?

3) They plays | are playing | playing computer games.

03 다음 질문에 대한 대답을 완성하시오.

1) Ⓐ Are you having ice cream? Ⓑ No, _____.

2) Ⓐ Is your mother cooking? Ⓑ Yes, _____.

3) Ⓐ Is it snowing now? Ⓑ No, _____.

1) have 먹다

04 주어진 동사를 이용하여 현재형이나 현재진행형 문장으로 쓰시오.

1) Look! The birds _____ a song in the tree. (sing)

2) She _____ the window on Sundays. (clean)

3) Ⓐ Is Karen sleeping now?

Ⓑ No, she isn't. She _____ in her diary in her room. (write)

2) on Sundays
일요일마다

3) write in one's diary
일기를 쓰다

05 다음 우리말을 영작하시오.

1) 그는 사진을 찍고 있다.

→ _____

2) 너는 내 말을 듣고 있지 않아.

→ _____

1) take a picture
사진을 찍다

2) listen to ~을 듣다

내신 족집게 문제

01 빈칸에 들어갈 알맞은 것을 고르시오.

He _____ his hair every day.

① wash   ② washs   ③ is wash
④ washes   ⑤ is washing

02 빈칸에 들어갈 수 <u>없는</u> 것을 고르시오.

_____ have a cute sister.

① I   ② He   ③ You
④ We   ⑤ They

03 빈칸에 들어갈 알맞은 것을 고르시오.

_____ goes to school every day.

① We   ② My friends   ③ Your brother
④ You   ⑤ Sumi and Mimi

04 대화의 빈칸에 들어갈 알맞은 것을 고르시오.

A: Do Amy and Janet play tennis on Sunday?
B: No, _____.

① she does   ② she doesn't   ③ they do
④ they don't   ⑤ we don't

05 다음 중 올바른 문장을 고르시오.

① My sister studys math hard.
② Karen doesn't has a new car.
③ Chris watching a cartoon on TV.
④ My sister doesn't her homework.
⑤ The birds are flying over the tree.

06 빈칸에 들어갈 알맞은 것을 고르시오.

He _____ drinking milk.

① doesn't   ② isn't   ③ don't
④ aren't   ⑤ am not

07 빈칸에 들어갈 단어를 순서대로 바르게 짝지은 것을 고르시오.

- He _____ the violin every morning.
- Look at the boy. He _____ the violin on the street.

① play – play   ② plays – play
③ play – plays   ④ is playing – play
⑤ plays – is playing

08 대화의 빈칸에 들어갈 알맞은 것을 고르시오.

A: Is Lucy cleaning the room?
B: _____. She is playing a computer game.

① Yes, he is   ② No, she isn't
③ Yes, she is   ④ No, she is
⑤ No, she doesn't

09 빈칸에 들어갈 알맞은 것을 고르시오.

Mina _____ a cell phone.

① isn't has   ② don't have   ③ doesn't has
④ don't   ⑤ doesn't have

10 빈칸에 들어갈 수 <u>없는</u> 것을 고르시오.

_____ doesn't read a newspaper.

① My mother   ② She   ③ They
④ Sumi   ⑤ My friend

11 다음 중 올바른 문장을 고르시오.

① They aren't make a card now.
② Karen doesn't cleaning the bathroom now.
③ The train is arriving at Seoul Station soon.
④ My father is having a brand-new cell phone.
⑤ Susan and Mike is singing a song on the stage.

12 대화의 빈칸에 들어갈 알맞은 것을 고르시오.

A: Do you brush your teeth three times a day?
B: Yes, _____.

① I don't   ② I am   ③ I am not
④ I do   ⑤ you do

[13-14] 밑줄 친 부분을 괄호 안의 단어로 바꾸어 문장을 다시 쓰시오.

13 They do their homework after school. (He)

→ _____

14 I speak Japanese very well. (My sister)

→ _____

15 밑줄 친 단어의 의미가 서로 같은 것을 고르시오.

① Chris looks like her mother.
   Chris doesn't like skiing.
② She is a very kind girl.
   She has many kinds of books.
③ He writes a letter to me.
   He writes a book.
④ Karen has a small cat.
   Karen has milk and pancakes for breakfast.
⑤ My sister does the dishes.
   My sister does not do the dishes in the evening.

16 대화의 빈칸에 들어갈 알맞은 것을 고르시오.

A: Does your brother like apples?
B: _____. He likes pears.

① Yes, he is   ② No, he isn't
③ Yes, he does   ④ No, he doesn't
⑤ Yes, he doesn't

17 다음 중 문장을 지시대로 바르게 바꾼 것을 고르시오.

① He is writing an email.
   의문문 Does he writing an email?
② She has a sister.
   의문문 Does she have a sister?
③ Your dog is sleeping.
   의문문 Is your dog sleep?
④ His sister is feeding the dog now.
   부정문 His sister isn't feed the dog now.
⑤ My mother drinks coffee alone.
   부정문 My mother doesn't drinks coffee alone.

[18-20] 우리말과 일치하도록 빈칸에 알맞은 말을 쓰시오.

18 그와 그녀는 일찍 일어나지 않는다.

→ He and she _____ _____ up early.

19 너는 교회에 가는 중이니?

→ _____ you _____ to church?

20 너의 아버지는 일요일 아침에 축구를 하시니?

→ _____ your father _____ soccer on Sunday morning?

정답 및 해설 p.5

01 다음 글의 밑줄 친 부분 중 어법상 틀린 것을 고르시오.

It ① is the eve of Chuseok. My mom ② is making Songpyeon in the kitchen. My dad ③ is sweeping the yard. My sister ④ is helping my mom now but I am playing computer games. I ⑤ am usually helping my dad but today I have a cold. I should stay in bed.

■ eve 전날 ■ Chuseok 추석 ■ Songpyeon 송편
■ sweep 빗자루로 쓸다 ■ yard 뜰, 마당

01 Karen의 주간 계획표를 보고 다음 문장을 완성하시오.

Monday	Have an English class
Tuesday	Visit grandmother
Wednesday	Take a piano lesson
Thursday	Do homework
Friday	Have an English class
Saturday	Take a trip
Sunday	Take a trip

Karen has English classes on Monday and Friday. On Tuesday, she _____ _____ _____. The next day, she _____ _____ _____ _____. On Thursday, she _____ _____ _____. On Saturday and Sunday, she _____ _____ _____.

02 다음 빈칸에 들어갈 말로 가장 적절한 것을 고르시오.

My sister Karen is a student. She goes to middle school. She **A** _____ in the first grade. She likes flowers, so she grows many kinds of flowers. Every day she **B** _____ them. Today she is sick, so I am **C** _____ them now.

■ grow 기르다, 재배하다 ■ kind 종류

	A		B		C
①	is	–	water	–	water
②	has	–	waters	–	waters
③	is	–	waters	–	watering
④	has	–	waters	–	watering
⑤	is	–	water	–	watering

02 다음 우리말을 읽고 바르게 영작하시오.

수미는 일요일마다 일찍 일어난다. 그녀는 아침을 먹고 도봉산을 등산하러 간다. 그 산은 늘 멋지다. 그녀는 산 정상에서 점심을 먹는다. 그리고 4시에 산에서 내려온다.

_____

_____

_____

_____

■ Mt. Dobong 도봉산 ■ wonderful 멋진, 훌륭한
■ on the top of a mountain 산 정상에서

Chapter 03

명사와 관사

Chapter 미리보기

셀 수 있는 명사의 복수형	cars, buses, cities, boys, knives, men, teeth
단수와 복수가 같은 명사	fish, sheep, deer
항상 복수형인 명사	shoes, pants, jeans, glasses, scissors
셀 수 없는 명사의 수량 표현	a cup of tea, a glass of water, a piece of cake
명사의 소유격	my friend's bag, the boys' bags, the legs of the chair
부정관사	a book, a university, an apple, an hour
정관사	the moon, the sun, the piano

Birds of a feather flock together. 같은 깃털을 가진 새들은 함께 모인다.

▶ 비슷한 유형의 사람들은 함께 모인다. (유유상종)

단수명사와 복수명사

A 셀 수 있는 명사

수를 셀 수 있는 명사 (ex) book, chair, house, pen, table)는 단수 또는 복수로 사용된다.
단수로 쓰일 때는 a 또는 an과 함께 사용된다.

Tips
• 예외
piano → pianos
photo → photos
roof → roofs

1 셀 수 있는 명사의 복수형

ⓐ 대부분의 명사 뒤에 -s를 붙인다.	car → cars, apple → apples
ⓑ -s, -ss, -sh, -ch, -x, -o로 끝나는 명사는 -es를 붙인다.	bus → buses, church → churches, box → boxes, potato → potatoes
ⓒ 〈자음 + -y〉로 끝나는 명사는 y를 i로 고치고 -es를 붙인다.	city → cities, baby → babies
ⓓ 〈모음 + -y〉로 끝나는 명사는 -s를 붙인다.	boy → boys, day → days, toy → toys
ⓔ -f, -fe로 끝나는 명사는 f, fe를 v로 고치고 -es를 붙인다.	leaf → leaves, knife → knives
ⓕ 단수와 복수의 형태가 같은 경우	sheep, deer, fish
ⓖ 복수에 -s를 붙이지 않는 경우 (불규칙 복수형)	man → men, tooth → teeth, child → children, mouse → mice

2 항상 복수형인 명사 : 짝을 이루는 명사로 a pair of 등을 사용하여 수를 센다.

a pair of	shoes, glasses, scissors, gloves, pants

B 셀 수 없는 명사

추상명사 (ex) love, information), 고유명사 (ex) Seoul, Lee, Korea), 물질명사 (ex) juice, cheese, paper)를 말하며 부정관사 a, an과 함께 사용할 수 없다.

▶ 셀 수 없는 명사의 수량 표현

two cups of coffee/tea   a bottle of beer/wine
a glass of water/milk/juice   a piece of cake/paper/cheese
a loaf of bread   a pair of shoes/gloves

Tips
• 소유대명사
(= 소유격 + 명사)
This is Tim's bag.
= This bag is Tim's.

⊕ 명사의 소유격

생물	단수명사 + 's	my friend's house
	복수명사가 -s로 끝나는 경우 → s'	the boys' coats
	복수명사가 -s로 끝나지 않은 경우 → 's	the children's books
무생물	of 사용	the legs of the piano

▽ ▲ ▽ ▲ ▽
Grammar Check-Up

O1 다음 명사의 복수형을 쓰시오.

1) box   – _____   2) boy   – _____

3) child   – _____   4) fish   – _____

5) sheep – _____   6) woman – _____

7) city   – _____   8) tooth   – _____

O2 다음 중 알맞은 것을 고르시오.

1) There is   a glass of | two glass of   water.

2) She drank   a cups of | two cups of   green tea.

3) We had   a loaf of | three pieces of   cake.

2) green tea 녹차

O3 다음 문장의 <u>틀린</u> 부분에 밑줄을 긋고 바르게 고쳐 쓰시오.

1) She has two pianoes in her house.   (→ _____)

2) I saw three deers.   (→ _____)

3) She visited her childrens' school.   (→ _____)

2) deer 사슴
3) visit 방문하다

O4 우리말과 일치하도록 빈칸에 알맞은 말을 쓰시오.

1) 그는 두 발을 다쳤다.

  → He hurt his _____.

2) 그녀는 청바지가 두 벌 있다.

  → She has two _____ of jeans.

3) 여자 아이들의 코트들이 매우 인기 있다.

  → The _____ _____ are very popular.

4) 그녀는 종이 세 장이 필요하다.

  → She needs _____ paper.

1) hurt 다치다
2) jeans 청바지
3) popular 인기 있는

07 관사

A 부정관사 a, an

부정관사 a, an은 셀 수 있는 단수명사 앞에 사용하며 '특정하지 않은 하나'라는 의미를 나타낸다.
복수명사나 셀 수 없는 명사와 함께 사용하지 않는다. 자음으로 발음되는 단어 앞에는 a를 쓰고
모음으로 발음되는 단어 앞에는 an을 쓴다.

a + 자음	a book, a pen, a chair, a cat, a dog, a university ＊ university는 철자가 모음 u로 시작해도 자음으로 발음되어 부정관사 a 사용
an + 모음 (a, e, i, o, u)	an apple, an elephant, an opera, an hour ＊ hour는 철자가 자음 h로 시작해도 모음으로 발음되어 부정관사 an 사용

1 '하나'라는 의미

ex I need a pen.

2 '～마다 (= per)'라는 의미

ex She goes to the library twice a week.

B 정관사 the

셀 수 있는 명사와 셀 수 없는 명사 앞에서 사용한다.

1 이미 나온 명사를 다시 언급할 때 사용한다.

ex She has a car. The car is expensive.

2 서로 알고 있는 것을 언급할 때 사용한다.

ex Open the door, please.

3 이 세상에서 유일한 것에 사용한다.

ex the moon, the sun, the earth, the sky, the sea

4 악기 이름 앞에 사용한다.

ex He can play the piano, the violin, and the flute.

⊕ 운동경기, 식사, 교통수단은 관사 없이 쓴다.

ex • He plays football/basketball/baseball.
• Did you have breakfast/lunch/dinner?
• I go to school by bus/taxi/train.

Grammar Check-Up

O1 다음 중 알맞은 것을 고르시오.

1) James rides a | an bike on weekends.

2) She waited him for a | an hour.

3) Ann plays a | the violin after school.

4) He entered a | an university in London.

O2 빈칸에 들어갈 알맞은 관사를 쓰시오. 관사가 필요치 않으면 X 표시하시오.

1) She studies English three hours _____ day.

2) We can go to _____ moon some day.

3) I'm reading a book. _____ book is really funny.

4) I don't usually eat _____ breakfast.

O3 다음 문장의 <u>틀린</u> 부분에 밑줄을 긋고 바르게 고쳐 쓰시오.

1) She plays the basketball with her friends.   (→ _____)

2) He eats a egg for breakfast.   (→ _____)

3) The moon moves around an earth.   (→ _____)

O4 우리말과 일치하도록 빈칸에 알맞은 말을 쓰시오.

1) 나는 일요일마다 그와 함께 축구를 한다.

→ I play _____ _____ _____ on Sundays.

2) 하늘을 봐.

→ Look at _____ _____ .

3) 그녀는 일주일에 두 번 그를 만난다.

→ She meets him _____ _____ _____ .

내신 족집게 문제

01 명사의 단수형과 복수형이 바르게 짝지어진 것을 고르시오.

① city – citys   ② child – childs

③ sheep – sheeps   ④ mouse – mice

⑤ potato – potatos

02 빈칸에 들어갈 알맞은 것을 고르시오.

> There are _____ in the room.

① two knifes   ② two pianos   ③ two water

④ three boxs   ⑤ two babys

03 빈칸에 들어갈 수 <u>없는</u> 것을 고르시오.

> I gave her a _____.

① letter   ② hat   ③ book

④ pen   ⑤ umbrella

04 두 문장이 같은 뜻이 되도록 빈칸에 알맞은 말을 쓰시오.

> This ring is Susan's.
> = This is _____ _____.

05 빈칸에 들어갈 알맞은 것을 고르시오.

> There is a puppy. _____ puppy is so cute.

① A   ② An   ③ The

④ Those   ⑤ These

06 빈칸에 들어갈 수 <u>없는</u> 것을 고르시오.

> I have a pair of _____.

① scissors   ② jeans   ③ glasses

④ book   ⑤ shoes

07 빈칸에 알맞은 말이 바르게 짝지어진 것을 고르시오.

> • _____ university is near here.
> • Harry plays _____ cello on Sundays.

① A – a   ② An – a   ③ A – an

④ An – the   ⑤ A – the

08 빈칸에 들어갈 수 <u>없는</u> 것을 고르시오.

> This is _____ leg.

① my   ② Jane's   ③ Tim's

④ my sister's   ⑤ the table's

09 밑줄 친 부분의 쓰임이 <u>틀린</u> 것을 고르시오.

① There is <u>a</u> egg in the basket.

② He is <u>an</u> actor.

③ She ate <u>a</u> sandwich.

④ There is <u>a</u> cat under the table.

⑤ We play football once <u>a</u> week.

10 빈칸에 들어갈 알맞은 것을 고르시오.

> They have _____ water.

① a   ② a bottle of   ③ a piece of

④ a pair of   ⑤ a loaf of

[11-12] 우리말과 일치하도록 빈칸에 알맞은 말을 쓰시오.

11

그 의자의 다리들은 길다.

→ The _____ _____ _____

_____ are long.

12

이 소년들의 가방들은 초록색이다.

→ These _____ _____ are green.

13 다음 중 the가 들어갈 수 <u>없는</u> 문장을 고르시오.

① I can play _____ piano.

② _____ sun is shining.

③ Open _____ window, please.

④ There is a bag. _____ bag is his.

⑤ We went to the library by _____ bike.

14 빈칸에 들어갈 알맞은 단어를 <u>모두</u> 고르시오.

She gave him a piece of _____.

① milk   ② cake   ③ paper

④ coffee   ⑤ water

15 밑줄 친 부분이 어법상 <u>틀린</u> 것을 고르시오.

① He gave me <u>a pen</u>.

② She found <u>Tim's gloves</u>.

③ <u>The piano's legs</u> are short.

④ She is wearing <u>a pair of jeans</u>.

⑤ I drank <u>two glasses of apple juice</u>.

16 빈칸에 알맞은 말을 쓰시오.

There is a photo on the desk.

→ There are three _____ on the desk.

17 밑줄 친 부분 중 수량 표현이 올바른 것을 고르시오.

① I have <u>a pair of</u> cheese.

② She gave me <u>a cup of</u> paper.

③ He lost <u>a piece of</u> gloves.

④ There is <u>a piece of</u> cake.

⑤ I want to drink <u>a pair of</u> coffee.

18 빈칸에 들어갈 알맞은 것을 고르시오.

David bought _____.

① three bottles of wines

② threes bottle of wine

③ three bottles of wine

④ a pairs of gloves

⑤ a pair of glove

19 밑줄 친 부분이 어법상 <u>틀린</u> 것을 고르시오.

① <u>The</u> bag is mine.

② She can play <u>the</u> piano.

③ Close <u>the</u> door, please.

④ <u>The</u> sun rises in the east.

⑤ We play <u>the</u> baseball every day.

20 다음 중 올바른 문장을 고르시오.

① They live in the Canada.

② We go to school by the bike.

③ The news are shocking.

④ He only had a bowls of rice for lunch.

⑤ I have a book. The book is interesting.

정답 및 해설 **p.6**

O1 다음 글의 밑줄 친 부분 중 어법상 <u>틀린</u> 것을 고르시오.

> My dad bought ① <u>some</u> Christmas presents for us. I needed ② <u>a pair of glass</u>. So he bought them for me. He got ③ <u>a lot of</u> toys for my baby sister. My brother, Tim, wanted ④ <u>an</u> MP3 player. My dad went to a discount store. A shop assistant gave him ⑤ <u>a lot of</u> advice. So he bought a good one for Tim.

■ discount store 할인점　　■ shop assistant 가게 점원
■ advice 조언

O1 다음 그림을 보고 빈칸에 들어갈 알맞은 말을 쓰시오.

1) David is wearing ＿＿＿＿ ＿＿＿＿ white socks.

2) David is wearing ＿＿＿＿ ＿＿＿＿ glasses.

3) David is drinking ＿＿＿＿ ＿＿＿＿ tea.

O2 다음 괄호 안에서 어법에 맞는 표현으로 가장 적절한 것을 고르시오.

> Jane and I went to a bakery after we played **A**(the / ×) badminton. She ordered a piece of chocolate cake. She also wanted a glass of milk. I was hungry but I was going to have **B**(the / ×) dinner soon. So I just ordered a cup of tea. There we met Tim. He found a box of delicious cookies but it was too expensive. He didn't have much money, so he just bought **C**(a loaf of / a carton of) bread.

■ order 주문하다　　■ expensive 비싼

	A		**B**		**C**
①	the	–	×	–	a loaf of
②	the	–	the	–	a carton of
③	×	–	×	–	a loaf of
④	×	–	×	–	a carton of
⑤	×	–	the	–	a carton of

O2 다음 우리말을 읽고 바르게 영작하시오.

어제 우리 가족은 백화점에 갔다. 엄마는 장갑 한 켤레를 원하셨다. 나는 청바지 한 벌을 원했고, 내 남동생은 운동화 한 켤레를 원했다. 아빠는 단지 커피 한 잔 마시기를 원하셨다.

＿＿＿＿＿＿＿＿＿＿＿＿＿＿＿＿＿＿＿

＿＿＿＿＿＿＿＿＿＿＿＿＿＿＿＿＿＿＿

＿＿＿＿＿＿＿＿＿＿＿＿＿＿＿＿＿＿＿

＿＿＿＿＿＿＿＿＿＿＿＿＿＿＿＿＿＿＿

■ department store 백화점　　■ sneakers 운동화

Chapter 04

대명사

Chapter 미리보기

지시대명사	This/That is a book. These/Those are books. It is sunny/winter/May 10/8 o'clock/Friday.
재귀대명사	myself, yourself, himself, herself, ourselves, yourselves, themselves She loves herself. (재귀) I myself did it. (강조)
부정대명사	A: Do you have a pen? B: Yes, I have one. There are some books on the table. She doesn't have any pens..

Know thyself(= yourself).

▶ 너 자신을 알라.

08 지시대명사와 재귀대명사

A 지시대명사 this, that

Tips
• 지시형용사 + 명사
  This car is mine.
  I know that boy.

this는 가까이에 있는 대상을 가리키고 that은 멀리 있는 대상을 가리킨다.

	this (이것, 이 사람)	that (저것, 저 사람)
단수	This is a book. This is Jane.	That is a pen. That is Karen.
	these (이것들, 이 사람들)	those (저것들, 저 사람들)
복수	These are books. These are my friends.	Those are pens. Those are my sister's friends.

⊕ 의문문과 대답

ex
- A: Is this/that a book? 　B: Yes, it is. / No, it isn't.
- A: Are these/those books? 　B: Yes, they are. / No, they aren't.

B it

1 **지시대명사** : 앞에 나온 단수명사를 대신하여 it을 사용할 수 있다.

ex There is a coat on the desk. It is mine.

2 **it의 특별 용법 (비인칭주어)** : 다음과 같은 경우에 사용하며, '그것'이라고 해석하지 않는다.

시간, 요일, 날짜, 계절	It is nine/Sunday/May 1/winter.
날씨, 거리, 명암	It is sunny/2 kilometers/dark.

C 재귀대명사

'나 자신, 너(희들) 자신, 그(녀) 자신, 우리 자신, 그들 자신' 등으로 해석하며, 단수는 -self, 복수는 -selves를 붙여 사용한다.

	1인칭	2인칭	3인칭
단수	I → myself	you → yourself	he → himself, she → herself, it → itself
복수	we → ourselves	you → yourselves	they → themselves

1 **재귀적 용법** : 문장의 주어가 다시 목적어로 쓰이는 경우에는 재귀대명사를 쓰게 되는데, 이것을 재귀대명사의 재귀적 용법이라 하며 생략할 수 없다.

ex She loves herself.

2 **강조적 용법** : 명사, 대명사와 동격으로 쓰여 그 명사 또는 대명사를 강조한다. 강조할 단어의 뒤나 문장 맨 뒤에 위치하며 생략할 수 있다.

ex I (myself) did it. = I did it (myself).

Grammar Check-Up

01 밑줄 친 부분을 바르게 고쳐 쓰시오.

1) <u>These</u> is his book.   (→ _____)

2) <u>Those</u> car is theirs.   (→ _____)

3) <u>This</u> are her shoes.   (→ _____)

02 빈칸에 알맞은 지시대명사를 쓰시오.

1) _____ is summer.

2) **A** Is this your bag?   **B** No, _____ is Jina's.

3) **A** Are these his pants?   **B** Yes, _____ are his.

03 빈칸에 알맞은 재귀대명사를 쓰시오.

1) She is angry with _____.

2) They look at _____ in the mirror.

3) I made it _____.

1) be angry with
~에게 화나다

2) mirror 거울

04 다음 문장을 우리말로 해석하시오.

1) We love ourselves.

→ _____

2) These shoes are too big and those shoes are too small.

→ _____

05 다음 우리말을 영작하시오.

1) 저것들은 제인(Jane)의 모자들이다.

→ _____

2) 그는 직접 그것을 칠했다.

→ _____

2) paint 칠하다

Unit 09 부정대명사 one, some/any

A one

1 이미 나온 명사를 대신하여 단독으로 사용하는 경우

one	it
이미 앞에 나온 불특정한 명사를 대신하여 단독으로 사용 (= a + 명사)	이미 앞에 나온 특정한 명사를 대신하여 단독으로 사용 (= the + 명사)
A: Do you have a pen? B: Yes, I have <u>one</u>. (불특정한 명사에 사용) 　　= a pen	A: I read the book. B: I read <u>it</u>, too. (특정한 명사에 사용) 　　= the book

2 형용사 + one (단수) / 형용사 + ones (복수)

ex
- Which bag do you like, this <u>one</u> or that <u>one</u>?
　　　　　　　　　　　　(= this bag or that bag?)
- She has four puppies: a white <u>one</u>, and three black <u>ones</u>.
　　　　　　　　　　(= puppy)　　　　　(= puppies)

B some, any

some은 긍정문에 사용하고 any는 부정문과 의문문에 사용한다. 단, 권유를 나타내는 의문문에는 some을 사용하기도 한다. '약간, 조금'이라는 의미를 갖는다.

	긍정문	부정문	의문문
some	○	×	× (예외: 권유)
any	×	○	○

ex
- I have many foreign friends. Some are from Italy.
- He doesn't trust any of us.
- Did any of your friends come?

─⊕ some, any는 명사 앞에서 '약간의, 조금의'라는 의미를 가진 형용사로 쓰이기도 한다.

ex
- She has some books.
- Does she have any brothers or sisters?
- Would you like some ice cream? → 권유를 나타내는 의문문에서는 some 사용 가능

▽ ▲ ▽ ▲ ▽
Grammar Check-Up

정답 및 해설 **p.7**

O1 다음 중 알맞은 것을 고르시오.

1) I need a towel. Do you have   it | one ?

2)   Any | Some   of the books are interesting.

3) This watch is for you. Do you like   it | one ?

4) Does she have   any | some   concert tickets?

1) towel 수건

4) concert 음악회

O2 다음 문장의 틀린 부분에 밑줄을 긋고 바르게 고쳐 쓰시오.

1) Do you have some hats?   (→ _____)

2) I don't eat something after 9 p.m.   (→ _____)

3) There are any chairs in the room.   (→ _____)

4) Any of my classmates are from Canada.   (→ _____)

O3 밑줄 친 부분이 의미하는 것을 찾아 쓰시오.

1) Do you have a hairpin? I need <u>one</u>.   (→ _____)

2) She likes the movie. He likes <u>it</u>, too.   (→ _____)

3) I don't like red pants. Do you have black <u>ones</u>?   (→ _____)

1) hairpin 머리핀

O4 some 또는 any를 사용하여 다음 우리말을 영작하시오.

1) 나는 몇 명의 외국인 친구가 있다.

→ _____

2) 쿠키 좀 먹을래요?

→ _____

3) 나는 설탕이 좀 필요해요. 좀 가지고 있나요?

→ _____

1) foreign 외국의

3) sugar 설탕

O1 다음 중 it의 쓰임이 다른 하나를 고르시오.

① It is 8:00 p.m.　　② It is winter.
③ It is mine.　　④ It is sunny.
⑤ It is Monday.

O2 빈칸에 알맞은 단어를 순서대로 바르게 짝지은 것을 고르시오.

• A: Is that a suitcase?
  B: Yes, _____ is.
• A: Are those rings?
  B: Yes, _____ are.

① that – those　　② that – they
③ that – that　　④ it – they
⑤ it – those

O3 빈칸에 들어갈 단어가 다른 하나를 고르시오.

① _____ is rainy.
② Kate has _____.
③ _____ is spring.
④ _____ is hers.
⑤ _____ are your gloves.

O4 빈칸에 알맞은 단어를 순서대로 바르게 짝지은 것을 고르시오.

• The baby wants a toy. Do you have _____?
• I gave him the painting. He liked _____ very much.

① it – one　② this – that　③ one – it
④ that – this　⑤ it – it

O5 두 문장이 같은 뜻이 되도록 빈칸에 알맞은 말을 쓰시오.

He has no email address.
= He doesn't have _____ email address.

[06 - 08] 우리말과 일치하도록 빈칸에 알맞은 말을 쓰시오.

O6 나는 빵을 조금 가지고 있다.

→ I have _____ bread.

O7 나는 돈을 가지고 있지 않다.

→ I don't have _____ money.

O8 당신은 여기에 친구가 있습니까?

→ Do you have _____ friends here?

O9 밑줄 친 부분이 어법상 틀린 것을 고르시오.

① She cooked it herself.
② She talks to herself.
③ I am proud of myself.
④ He likes himself.
⑤ They themself cleaned the room.

10 밑줄 친 재귀대명사 중 생략할 수 있는 것을 고르시오.

① She loves herself.
② I talked to myself.
③ We know ourselves well.
④ He takes care of himself.
⑤ He made the jeans himself.

11 대화의 빈칸에 알맞은 단어를 순서대로 바르게 짝지은
것을 고르시오.

> A: Do you have _____ questions?
> B: Yes, I have _____ questions.

① some – some　　　② some – any

③ any – some　　　④ any – any

⑤ one – ones

12 다음 중 어색한 문장을 고르시오.

① He had dinner by himself.

② Those pencils are mine.

③ She doesn't have any friends.

④ Some like English and others like math.

⑤ There is a boat in the river. It's color is blue.

[13-14] 밑줄 친 부분 중 어법상 틀린 것을 고르시오.

13
Those books is written in English.
　①　　②　③　④　⑤

14
This is my friend's lunch box. They is empty.
　①　②　　③　　　　　④　⑤

15 보기의 밑줄 친 that과 쓰임이 같은 하나를 고르시오.

> 보기 That coat is Tim's.

① That is my sister's book.

② Is that his jacket?

③ That is Jane's house.

④ That car is very expensive.

⑤ Is that your mother?

16 밑줄 친 one이 언급하는 것을 찾아 쓰시오.

> My friend has a new MP3 player. She can
> listen to music and study English with it.
> I want to buy one. (→ _____)

17 대화의 빈칸에 알맞은 단어를 순서대로 바르게 짝지은
것을 고르시오.

> A: Which one is better?
> B: _____ is better than _____.

① These – that one

② This one – those one

③ These – those

④ This – that

⑤ Those ones – these ones

18 복수형 문장을 단수형 문장으로 바꾸어 쓰시오.

Those are Jane's books.

→ _____

19 다음 중 어색한 문장을 고르시오.

① She doesn't have any food.

② I lost some money.

③ Do you have some pens?

④ Would you like some cake?

⑤ They didn't get any presents.

20 밑줄 친 부분에 공통으로 들어갈 알맞은 것을 고르시오.

> • Would you like _____ orange juice?
> • There are _____ magazines on the table.

① any　　　② an　　　③ a

④ some　　　⑤ the

01 다음 글의 밑줄 친 부분 중 어법상 틀린 것을 고르시오.

> Jane wanted to read ① some books. But she didn't have ② any books. There were ③ any books on the desk. She asked me if she could read ④ those books. I told her that ⑤ they were not mine but my sister's. I also told her that I could lend her some of mine.

■ lend 빌려주다

02 다음 괄호 안에서 어법에 맞는 표현으로 가장 적절한 것을 고르시오.

> Tim : I need a bag.
> Do you have Ⓐ(one / it)?
> David : No, I don't.
> Look. There are some bags.
> Are those Jane's bags?
> Tim : No. Ⓑ(Those / They) are Paul's.
> He made them Ⓒ(myself / himself).

	Ⓐ		Ⓑ		Ⓒ
①	it	–	Those	–	himself
②	it	–	They	–	himself
③	one	–	They	–	myself
④	one	–	Those	–	myself
⑤	one	–	They	–	himself

01 다음 그림을 보고 some 또는 any를 사용하여 문장을 완성하시오.

1) There _____ _____ _____ on the table.

2) She _____ _____ _____ money.

3) He _____ _____ pens.

02 다음 우리말을 읽고 바르게 영작하시오.

나는 책을 몇 권 가지고 있다. 이것들은 소설책이고, 저것들은 자서전이다. 그리고 나는 잡지도 한 권 가지고 있다. 그것은 영어 잡지이다. 나는 만화책은 가지고 있지 않다.

_____

_____

_____

_____

_____

■ novel 소설책　■ biography 자서전
■ magazine 잡지　■ comic book 만화책

Chapter 05

형용사와 부사

Chapter 미리보기

형용사	nice, kind, happy → 명사 수식
부사	nicely, kindly, happily → 형용사, 부사, 동사, 문장 수식
빈도부사	always, usually, often, sometimes, never → be동사나 조동사 뒤, 일반동사 앞에 위치
원급	as + 형용사/부사 원급 + as
비교급	형용사/부사 + -er
최상급	형용사/부사 + -est

The more, the better.

▶ 많으면 많을수록 좋다. (다다익선)

10 형용사, 부사, 빈도부사

A 형용사

형용사는 명사를 수식하거나 주어나 목적어의 보어 역할을 하며, '~한'으로 해석된다.

1 형용사 + 명사 : 주로 명사나 대명사를 앞에서 수식한다.

ex He is a good student.

2 something/anything/nothing + 형용사

ex She saw something big.

3 보어 : 주어나 목적어를 보충 설명한다.

ex • He is nice. (주격 보어)　　　　　　　• She made me happy. (목적격 보어)

B 부사

형용사, 동사, 다른 부사 또는 문장 전체를 수식하며, '~하게'로 해석된다.

1 부사 만들기 : 대부분의 부사는 〈형용사 + -ly〉로 만들고, -y로 끝나는 형용사는 y를 i로 고치고 -ly를 붙인다.

형용사 + -ly	slow → slowly, nice → nicely, quick → quickly, careful → carefully
-y로 끝난 경우 : y → i + ly	happy → happily, easy → easily, angry → angrily
형용사와 부사가 같은 경우	fast, hard, early, late

ex • He is a fast runner.　　　　　　• He runs fast.
　　빠른(형용사)　　　　　　　　　　빠르게(부사)

Tips
• too vs. either
'~ 또한'이라는 의미를 나타낸다. too는 긍정문에 쓰고 either는 부정문에 쓴다.

2 부사의 역할 : 형용사, 동사, 다른 부사, 문장 전체 등을 수식한다.

ex • They speak slowly. (동사 수식)　　　　• He is very tall. (형용사 수식)
　• She did it very well. (부사 수식)　　　• Unfortunately, she died. (문장 수식)

C 빈도부사

얼마나 자주 일어나는 일인지를 나타낼 때 사용한다. be동사나 조동사의 뒤, 일반동사의 앞에 위치한다.

Tips
• 조동사 : can, will, may, must 등
▶ Chapter 09 참조

be동사 + 빈도부사	She is	always (항상) usually (대개) often (종종) sometimes (때때로) never (결코 ~않다)	happy.
조동사 + 빈도부사	She can		help him.
빈도부사 + 일반동사	She		smiles.

Grammar Check-Up

정답 및 해설 p.8

01 다음 중 알맞은 것을 고르시오.

1) He drives his car very   careful ∣ carefully .

2) They   go often ∣ often go   to the movies.

3) She saw a very   beautiful ∣ beautifully   girl on the street.

1) careful 조심성 있는

3) go to the movies
   영화 보러 가다

02 주어진 단어를 알맞게 배열하여 올바른 문장을 쓰시오.

1) (are, always, they, kind)

→ _____

2) (very, speaks, she, English, well)

→ _____

3) (will, it, read, Jane, never)

→ _____

03 다음 문장의 틀린 부분에 밑줄을 긋고 바르게 고쳐 쓰시오.

1) This is special nothing.   (→ _____)

2) He usually is nice.   (→ _____)

3) They lived happy.   (→ _____)

04 다음 문장을 우리말로 해석하시오.

1) He is a quiet boy.   → _____

2) He speaks quietly.   → _____

05 다음 우리말을 영작하시오.

1) 나는 빨리 먹는다.   → _____

2) 그는 항상 친절하다.   → _____

11 형용사의 비교급과 최상급

A 원급 비교 (as + 형용사/부사의 원급 + as)

두 대상을 비교하여 양쪽이 동등하게 '…만큼 ~한'

ex
- Jane is as clever as Henry.
  형용사
- Harry walks as slowly as David.
  부사

⊕ 원급 비교의 부정은 두 대상을 비교하여 그 차이를 나타낸다.

ex • A bus is not as fast as a car = A car is faster than a bus.

B 비교급 (비교급 + than)

두 대상을 비교하여 '어느 한 쪽이 더 ~한'

ex
- Jane is taller than Harry.
- David is more popular than Jane.

⊕ 비교급 강조

| Jane is | much, far, even, a lot, still (훨씬) | taller than Harry. |

C 최상급 (the + 최상급)

셋 이상을 비교하여 '어느 하나가 가장 ~한'

ex • Harry is the smartest student in our class.   • Harry is the smartest student of all.

Tips
• 〈one of the + 최상급 +복수명사〉는 최상급 표현으로 '가장 ~한 것들 중 하나'라는 뜻이다.

D 형용사의 비교급과 최상급 만들기

	형용사	비교급	최상급
1음절 : -er, -est를 붙인다.	old	older	oldest
1음절이 〈단모음 + 단자음〉으로 끝난 경우 마지막 자음을 한 번 더 쓰고 -er, -est를 붙인다.	big hot	bigger hotter	biggest hottest
-y로 끝난 경우 y를 i로 고치고 -er, -est를 붙인다.	easy	easier	easiest
-ful, -ous, -ing, -less로 끝나는 2음절이나 3음절 이상의 형용사는 앞에 more, most를 붙인다.	beautiful	more beautiful	most beautiful
불규칙 변화	good/well bad many/much	better worse more	best worst most

Grammar Check-Up

정답 및 해설 p.8

O1 주어진 단어의 비교급이나 최상급을 이용하여 문장을 완성하시오.

1) Sarah is _____ than Jane. (healthy)

2) This is _____ of all. (expensive)

3) They ran _____ than us. (fast)

4) Tim is _____ student in our class. (strong)

1) healthy 건강한

O2 다음 단어의 비교급과 최상급을 쓰시오.

1) big － _____ － _____

2) good － _____ － _____

3) important － _____ － _____

O3 다음 문장의 <u>틀린</u> 부분에 밑줄을 긋고 바르게 고쳐 쓰시오.

1) David is more older than Tim.　　　　(→ _____)

2) Tim is as smarter as David.　　　　(→ _____)

2) smart 영리한

O4 다음 문장을 우리말로 해석하시오.

1) This question is much easier than that one.

→ _____

2) He is the most popular football player in Korea.

→ _____

1) question 질문
2) popular 인기 있는

O5 다음 우리말을 영작하시오.

1) 팸(Pam)은 데이비드(David)만큼 친절하다.

→ _____

2) 이 학교는 우리 마을에서 가장 오래된 학교이다.

→ _____

2) town 마을

O1 밑줄 친 빈도부사의 위치가 잘못된 것을 고르시오.

① She is <u>always</u> kind.

② He eats <u>usually</u> lunch at 1 p.m.

③ They will <u>never</u> come back.

④ I <u>often</u> visit him.

⑤ I can <u>sometimes</u> help you.

O2 다음 중 어법상 틀린 문장을 고르시오.

① I arrived home late.　　② He studied hard.

③ We walked quietly.　　④ She ran fastly.

⑤ They drive their cars carefully.

O3 다음 중 '원급 – 비교급 – 최상급'의 연결이 잘못된 것을 고르시오.

① easy – easier – easiest

② thin – thiner – thinest

③ many – more – most

④ cheap – cheaper – cheapest

⑤ interesting – more interesting
　　– most interesting

O4 빈칸에 들어갈 알맞은 것을 고르시오.

This chocolate is as _____ as that one.

① sweeter　　② more sweet　　③ sweet

④ sweetest　　⑤ most sweet

O5 다음 짝지어진 관계가 잘못된 것을 고르시오.

① well – better　　　② cold – colder

③ cool – cooler　　　④ many – manier

⑤ beautiful – more beautiful

O6 빈칸에 들어갈 수 <u>없는</u> 것을 고르시오.

Susan sang _____ louder than Tim.

① a lot　　② much　　③ very

④ even　　⑤ far

[07-08] 빈칸에 들어갈 알맞은 것을 고르시오.

O7

She went to the concert yesterday. He went there, _____.

① either　　② neither　　③ so

④ too　　⑤ much

O8

He didn't finish his homework. She didn't finish it, _____.

① either　　② neither　　③ never

④ too　　⑤ so

O9 다음 표의 내용과 일치하지 않는 것을 고르시오.

	height	weight
Suji	160cm	53kg
Mina	165cm	53kg
Yoon	150cm	53kg

① Mina is taller than Yoon.

② Mina is as heavy as Suji.

③ Yoon is as heavy as Suji.

④ Suji is as tall as Mina.

⑤ Yoon is much shorter than Mina.

10 다음 중 어법상 <u>틀린</u> 문장을 고르시오.

① Tim eats often pizza.

② That color is brighter than this one.

③ Jane cries more than Gina does.

④ Suji talks less than June does.

⑤ This is the most expensive cap in this store.

11 빈칸에 들어갈 수 <u>없는</u> 것을 고르시오.

This one is _____ than that one.

① lighter   ② heavier   ③ colder

④ best   ⑤ fresher

12 밑줄 친 부분의 쓰임이 나머지와 <u>다른</u> 하나를 고르시오.

① He ate <u>too</u> much.

② It is <u>too</u> expensive.

③ I like it, <u>too</u>.

④ The bag is <u>too</u> heavy.

⑤ The room is <u>too</u> crowded.

[13-15] 주어진 단어를 알맞은 형태로 바꾸어 빈칸에 쓰시오.

13

Jane has 1,000 won and Tim has 2,000 won.

→ Tim has _____ money than Jane has.
              (much)

14

Tim speaks English _____ than I do. (well)

15

Which is _____, an elephant or a rabbit?
         (big)

[16-17] 두 문장이 같은 뜻이 되도록 빈칸에 알맞은 말을 쓰시오.

16

The man is a careful driver.

= The man drives _____.

17

The woman is a good singer.

= The woman sings _____.

[18-19] 주어진 빈도부사를 알맞은 위치에 넣어 문장을 다시 쓰시오.

18 She is absent from school. (never)

→ _____

19 My friend plays badminton. (often)

→ _____

20 두 문장의 뜻이 같지 <u>않은</u> 것을 고르시오.

① This car is more expensive than that one.
    = That car is cheaper than this one.

② Jane is not as tall as Tim.
    = Jane is taller than Tim.

③ The sun is even bigger than the earth.
    = The sun is much bigger than the earth.

④ Chris is as old as Karen.
    = Chris and Karen are the same age.

⑤ She dances very well.
    = She is a very good dancer.

정답 및 해설 p.9

O1 다음 글의 밑줄 친 부분 중 어법상 틀린 것을 고르시오.

> John is ① a twelve-year-old boy. He has
> ② one brother Paul. John and Paul ③ play
> soccer very well. They are going to join the
> national junior team this summer. Paul has
> ④ a lot of fans but John has few fans. Paul is
> ⑤ very more popular than John.

■ national team 국가대표팀　　■ few 거의 없는

O1 다음 그림을 보고 형용사 expensive를 이용하여 빈칸에 알맞은 말을 쓰시오.

1) Susan's bag is not as _____ as Tim's book.

2) Tim's shoes are _____ _____ than Susan's.

3) Tim's book is _____ _____ _____ of all.

O2 다음 우리말을 읽고 바르게 영작하시오.

데이비드(David)와 나는 자주 축구를 같이 한다. 그는 우리 코치보다 키가 크다. 그는 나보다 훨씬 키가 크다. 그는 우리 축구부에서 키가 제일 크다. 하지만 나는 그만큼 힘이 세다.

_____

_____

_____

_____

■ coach 코치　　■ soccer team 축구부

O2 다음 괄호 안에서 어법에 맞는 표현으로 가장 적절한 것을 고르시오.

> David and Tim are in the same class. David
> Ⓐ (always is / is always) busy but he often
> helps others. Tim is busy, Ⓑ (either / too) but
> he never helps others. So their classmates
> like David very much and David has Ⓒ (many /
> more) friends than Tim has.

	Ⓐ		Ⓑ		Ⓒ
①	always is	–	either	–	many
②	always is	–	too	–	more
③	always is	–	either	–	more
④	is always	–	too	–	more
⑤	is always	–	either	–	many

Chapter 06

문장의 형식과 종류

Chapter 미리보기

1형식	주어 (~은, ~는, ~이, ~가) + 동사 (~다)	명령문	동사원형 (~해라)
2형식	주어 + 동사 + 보어 (주어를 보충 설명)	부정 명령문	Don't + 동사원형 (~하지 말아라)
3형식	주어 + 동사 + 목적어 (~을, ~를)	청유형 명령문	Let's + 동사원형 (~하자)
4형식	주어 + 동사 + 간접목적어 (~에게) + 직접목적어 (~을, ~를)	감탄문	What + a(n) + 형용사 + 명사 + 주어 + 동사!
5형식	주어 + 동사 + 목적어 + 목적격 보어		How + 형용사/부사 + 주어 + 동사!

Boys, be ambitious.

▶ 소년들이여, 야망을 가져라.

A 주어 + 동사 (1형식)

	주어	동사
그가 웃는다.	그가	웃는다
He laughs.	He	laughs

B 주어 + 동사 + 보어 (2형식)

	주어	동사	보어
그는 슬프다.	그는	이다	슬픈
He is sad.	He	is	sad

C 주어 + 동사 + 목적어 (3형식)

	주어	동사	목적어
캐런은 테니스를 친다.	캐런은	친다	테니스를
Karen plays tennis.	Karen	plays	tennis

D 주어 + 동사 + 간접목적어 + 직접목적어 (4형식)

	주어	동사	간접목적어	직접목적어
그는 나에게 꽃을 사 주었다.	그는	사 주었다	나에게	꽃을
He bought me flowers.	He	bought	me	flowers

E 주어 + 동사 + 목적어 + 목적격 보어 (5형식)

	주어	동사	목적어	목적격 보어
우리는 그를 크리스라고 부른다.	우리는	부른다	그를	크리스라고
We call him Chris.	We	call	him	Chris

Grammar Check-Up

정답 및 해설 p.10

01 보기와 같이 다음 문장을 문장 요소로 구분하여 표시하시오.

> **보기** <u>My father</u> <u>cooks</u>.
>   주어   동사

1) Karen eats breakfast.

2) She teaches us math.

3) My brother is a college student.

4) A bird is flying.

2) teach 가르치다
3) college 대학
4) fly 날다

02 우리말과 일치하도록 주어진 말을 바르게 배열하시오.

1) 그의 할머니는 미국에 살고 계신다. (lives, in America, his grandmother)

→ _____

2) 그들은 거리에서 에릭을 만났다. (Eric, on the street, they, met)

→ _____

3) 그들은 그녀를 가수로 만들었다. (her, a singer, made, they)

→ _____

2) meet (– met – met)
만나다

03 다음 우리말을 영작하시오.

1) 나의 가족은 그 강아지를 '해피'라고 부른다.

→ _____

2) 나의 부모님은 어제 그림 한 점을 사셨다.

→ _____

3) 너는 행복해 보인다.

→ _____

2) buy (– bought – bought)
사다

13 there is, there are

A 쓰임

there is 다음에는 단수명사가 오며, there are 다음에는 복수명사가 온다. 이때 there는 뜻이 없고
문장만 유도하므로 '유도부사'라고 한다.

> • There is + 단수명사 (~이 있다)
> • There are + 복수명사 (~들이 있다)

ex • There is a koala at the zoo.
　　 • There are some books on the desk.
　　 • There is a lot of milk in the refrigerator.

B 부정문

be동사 뒤에 not을 붙인다.

> • There is not ~ (= There isn't ~) (~이 없다)
> • There are not ~ (= There aren't ~) (~들이 없다)

ex • There is not a student in the classroom.
　　 • There are not many flowers in the garden.

C 의문문

be동사를 there 앞에 놓는다.

> • Is there + 단수명사 ~? (~이 있습니까?)
> • Are there + 복수명사 ~? (~들이 있습니까?)

ex • A: Is there any water in the bottle?　　B: Yes, there is. / No, there isn't.
　　 • A: Are there any glasses on the table?　　B: Yes, there are. / No, there aren't.

⊕ 유도부사와 지시부사 there

	유도부사 (there)	지시부사 (there)
뜻	없음	거기에, 저기에
예문	There is a toy car in the box.	He lives there.

Grammar Check-Up

정답 및 해설 p.10

O1 다음 중 알맞은 것을 고르시오.

1) There is | are a big tree in front of my house.

2) There is | are 11 players on a soccer team.

3) Is | Are there a drugstore near here?

4) There is | are a lot of sugar in this coffee.

O2 다음 질문에 대한 대답을 완성하시오.

1) Ⓐ Is there a letter for me?

   Ⓑ No, _____ _____.

2) Ⓐ Are there 5 players on a basketball team?

   Ⓑ Yes, _____ _____.

3) Ⓐ Is there any meat in the refrigerator?

   Ⓑ _____, _____ _____. You don't need to buy any.

O3 다음 문장을 우리말로 해석하시오.

1) There are a lot of people in the room.

   → _____

2) There isn't any juice in the bottle.

   → _____

O4 다음 우리말을 영작하시오.

1) 바구니 안에 양파 한 개가 있니?

   → _____

2) 그 공원에는 많은 나무들이 있다.

   → _____

14 명령문과 감탄문

A 명령문

주어 you를 생략하고 동사원형으로 시작한다. 정중한 표현을 써야 할 경우에는 문장의 앞이나 뒤에 please를 붙인다.

ex
- Close your eyes.
- Please have some bread. (= Have some bread, please.)
- Be happy.

B 부정 명령문

Don't를 문장 앞에 놓고 '~하지 말아라'라고 해석한다.

ex
- Don't be late.
- Don't cry.

Tips
- Let's dance.
  = Shall we dance?
  = How about
    dancing?
  = What about
    dancing?
- Let's는 Let us의
  줄임말

C 긍정·부정의 청유형 명령문

	긍정의 청유형 명령문	부정의 청유형 명령문
형태	Let's + 동사원형	Let's + not + 동사원형
뜻	~하자	~하지 말자

ex
- Let's eat out.
- Let's not eat out.

D 감탄문

기쁨, 놀람, 슬픔 등의 감정을 표현할 때 사용한다.

- What + a(n) + 형용사 + 명사 + 주어 + 동사!
- How + 형용사/부사 + 주어 + 동사!

ex
- What a good boy he is!
- How foolish you are!

⊕ 주어가 대명사이고, 동사가 be동사일 경우 주어와 동사는 생략이 가능하다.

ex
- She is a very beautiful woman. → What a beautiful woman (she is)!
- They are very clever boys. → What clever boys (they are)!

O1 다음 문장을 지시대로 바꾸어 쓰시오.

1) You are kind.

명령문 ▶ _____

2) You are not lazy.

부정 명령문 ▶ _____

3) Let's have bread for lunch.

부정문 ▶ _____

2) lazy 게으른

O2 다음 문장을 감탄문으로 바꾸어 쓰시오.

1) It is a very wonderful world.

→ _____

2) They are very good students.

→ _____

3) He swims very well.

→ _____

1) wonderful
   놀랄 만한, 훌륭한

O3 다음 문장을 우리말로 해석하시오.

1) Let's not speak Korean in class.

→ _____

2) What a beautiful day it is!

→ _____

O4 다음 우리말을 영작하시오.

1) 생일 파티를 열자.

→ _____

2) 하늘이 참 맑구나!

→ _____

2) clear 맑은

15 부가의문문

A 부가의문문 만들기

부가의문문이란 상대방의 동의나 확인을 구하기 위해 문장 뒤에 덧붙이는 의문문을 말한다.

1 앞 문장이 '긍정'이면 '부정'으로, '부정'이면 '긍정'으로 부가의문문을 만든다.

> **ex** • It is a beautiful day, isn't it?
> • She can't speak English, can she?

2 부가의문문의 주어는 대명사로 쓴다.

> **ex** • Karen speaks three languages, doesn't she?
> • The movie is very exciting, isn't it?

3 앞 문장이 be동사이거나 조동사일 때는 그대로 쓴다. 앞 문장에 일반동사의 현재형이 올 경우 do, does를 쓰고, 앞 문장에 일반동사의 과거형이 올 경우 did를 쓴다.

> **ex** • He was at home, wasn't he? (be동사)
> • He is playing soccer, isn't he? (진행형)
> • He won't be late, will he? (조동사)
> • He likes meat, doesn't he? (일반동사의 현재형)
> • He closed the window, didn't he? (일반동사의 과거형)

⊕ there is, there are 문장은 **there**로 부가의문문을 만든다.

> **ex** • There aren't any cars on the street, are there?

B 부가의문문의 대답

부가의문문의 대답은 일반 의문문의 대답과 같다.

> **ex** • A: She can speak English, can't she?　　B: Yes, she can. / No, she can't.

C 명령문의 부가의문문

일반 명령문의 부가의문문은 긍정문, 부정문에 상관없이 will you?를 쓰고, 청유형 명령문의 부가의문문은 shall we?를 쓴다.

> **ex** • Please lock the door, will you?
> • Don't drink milk, will you?
> • Let's play computer games, shall we?

Grammar Check-Up

01 다음 문장 뒤에 부가의문문을 쓰시오.

1) Your sister lost weight, _____?

2) He isn't washing his car, _____?

3) Your father works in a hospital, _____?

4) She will stop by the store, _____?

Note
1) lose weight 살을 빼다
4) stop by ~에 들르다

02 우리말과 일치하도록 빈칸에 알맞은 말을 쓰시오.

1) 날씨가 화창해, 그렇지 않아?

→ It is sunny, _____ _____?

2) 그는 지금 잠을 자고 있지 않아, 그렇지?

→ He _____ _____ now, is he?

3) 너의 어머니는 꽃을 매우 좋아하시는구나, 그렇지 않아?

→ Your mother _____ flowers very much, doesn't _____?

03 다음 문장의 틀린 부분에 밑줄을 긋고 바르게 고쳐 쓰시오.

1) There are two flies on the wall, aren't they?　(→ _____)

2) Your mother cooks well, isn't she?　(→ _____)

3) Rome isn't in Spain, is Rome?　(→ _____)

1) fly 파리

04 다음 우리말을 영작하시오.

1) 너는 피아노를 칠 수 있어, 그렇지 않아?

→ _____

2) 그녀는 생선을 좋아하지 않아, 그렇지?

→ _____

내신 족집게 문제

01 빈칸에 들어갈 알맞은 것을 고르시오.

> He sometimes drives too fast, _____?

① does he   ② isn't he   ③ doesn't he
④ is he   ⑤ didn't he

02 대화의 빈칸에 들어갈 알맞은 것을 고르시오.

> A: Is there any butter on the plate?
> B: No, _____.

① it isn't   ② it is   ③ there is
④ there isn't   ⑤ there aren't

03 빈칸에 공통으로 들어갈 알맞은 말을 쓰시오.

> • _____ beautiful flowers they are!
> • _____ an old hat this is!

04 대화의 빈칸에 들어갈 알맞은 것을 고르시오.

> A: Karen doesn't speak Korean, does she?
> B: Yes, _____. She speaks Korean very
>   well.

① she is   ② she does   ③ she doesn't
④ she isn't   ⑤ she did

05 다음 문장을 감탄문으로 바꾸어 쓰시오.

He is a very good singer.

→ _____

06 빈칸에 들어갈 알맞은 것을 고르시오.

> Mina is often late for school, _____?

① isn't Mina   ② isn't she   ③ is she
④ doesn't she   ⑤ didn't she

07 밑줄 친 부가의문문이 올바른 것을 고르시오.

① That is my key, isn't that?
② Let's go skiing, will you?
③ You won't be at home tonight, will you?
④ Your sister can sing well, can she?
⑤ There are not any flowers in the garden, are they?

08 빈칸에 들어갈 수 없는 것을 고르시오.

> There is _____ in the refrigerator.

① an apple   ② a bottle of milk
③ some bread   ④ a lot of eggs
⑤ a lot of water

09 두 문장의 뜻이 같도록 빈칸에 알맞은 말을 쓰시오.

> A lot of tall buildings are in Seoul.
> = _____ _____ a lot of tall
> buildings in Seoul.

10 다음 중 올바른 문장을 고르시오.

① What fast Karen runs!
② Not be shy.
③ I gave a pen Karen.
④ Karen, don't tell a lie!
⑤ How cute children they are!

11 다음 문장을 부정문으로 바꾸어 쓰시오.

Let's go out this evening.

→ _____

12 다음 중 올바른 문장을 고르시오.

① Let's don't take a shower.
② Please give me a coin, shall we?
③ The movie wasn't exciting, was it?
④ There are some cheese in the refrigerator.
⑤ Your father took a picture of the castle, doesn't he?

13 빈칸에 들어갈 알맞은 것을 고르시오.

Karen and Chris didn't work last Saturday, _____?

① did he   ② do we   ③ did they
④ didn't they   ⑤ don't they

[14-15] 우리말과 일치하도록 빈칸에 알맞은 말을 쓰시오.

14 너의 어머니는 참 친절하시구나!

→ _____ _____ your mother is!

15 그는 나에게 손목시계를 사 주었다.

· He bought _____

[16-17] 다음 문장 뒤에 알맞은 부가의문문을 쓰시오.

16 Shakespeare wrote *Romeo and Juliet*, _____?

17 Please, don't forget this number, _____?

18 빈칸에 들어갈 알맞은 것을 고르시오.

He made me pizza.
= He made pizza _____.

① to me   ② for me   ③ of me
④ with me   ⑤ on me

19 빈칸에 알맞은 단어를 순서대로 바르게 짝지은 것을 고르시오.

· There _____ a lot of children in the park.
· There _____ a lot of juice in the bottle.

① is – are   ② are – are   ③ is – is
④ are – am   ⑤ are – is

20 다음 문장을 지시대로 바꿀 때 틀린 문장을 고르시오.

① You are honest.
  명령문 Be honest.
② You listen to me.
  명령문 Listen to me.
③ She swims very well.
  감탄문 How well she swims!
④ There is a flower in the vase.
  부정문 There isn't a flower in the vase.
⑤ The movie is very exciting.
  감탄문 How exciting the movie!

정답 및 해설 p.11

O1 다음 글의 밑줄 친 부분 중 어법상 틀린 것을 고르시오.

> Minho : Welcome to my home.
> Karen : ① Thank you for inviting me.
> Minho : Have a seat. Help yourself.
> Karen : ② This is Kimchi, isn't it?
> Minho : That's right.
> Karen : ③ It's very hot, isn't it?
> Minho : Yes, a little. Try it.
> Karen : ④ It is good but hot. What is it?
> ⑤ How delicious is it!
> Minho : It's Bulgogi. I like it very much.

O1 다음 그림을 보고 감탄문을 쓰시오.

1)

What _____!

2)

How _____!

3)

_____!

O2 다음 빈칸에 들어갈 말로 가장 적절한 것을 고르시오.

> Miyeong : There are a lot of people here,
> Ⓐ_____?
> Intae : Yes, there are. On Sundays, many people ride bikes or take a walk here.
> Miyeong : It's so hot, Ⓑ_____?
> I am thirsty.
> Intae : Yes, it is. Let's take a rest and drink some water.
> Miyeong : Okay. There is a bench over there.

	Ⓐ		Ⓑ
①	are they	–	is it
②	aren't they	–	is it
③	are there	–	isn't it
④	aren't there	–	isn't it
⑤	are there	–	is it

O2 다음 우리말을 읽고 바르게 영작하시오.

수미 : 날씨 정말 좋다, 그렇지 않아?
미미 : 응, 그래. 수미야, 이 나비를 봐.
수미 : 나비가 정말 예쁘구나!
미미 : 이 꽃들을 봐. 정말 아름다워, 그렇지 않아?

Sumi : _____

Mimi : _____

Sumi : _____

Mimi : _____

_____

▪ butterfly 나비

Chapter 07

시제

Chapter 미리보기

	일반동사의 과거	현재완료
형태	동사원형 + -ed 또는 불규칙 변화	have/has + 과거분사
의미	과거의 동작이나 상태 표현	과거의 동작이나 상태가 현재까지 영향 (경험, 계속, 결과, 완료의 의미)
부정문	주어 + did + not + 동사원형	주어 + have/has + not + 과거분사
의문문	Did + 주어 + 동사원형 ～?	Have/Has + 주어 + 과거분사 ～?

Time flies like an arrow. 시간은 활처럼 날아간다.

▶ 시간은 쏜살같이 흐른다.

Unit 16 be동사의 과거형

A be동사의 과거형

was와 were가 있으며, 주로 과거의 상태를 표현한다. '~이었다, ~있었다'라고 해석한다.

- I/He/She/It + was
- We/You/They + Were

Tips
- 과거를 나타내는 표현
  ago ~전에
  last 지난
  yesterday 어제

ex ▶
- I was in the library yesterday.
- He was ten years old last year.
- They were at home last weekend.

B be동사 과거형의 부정문

〈was/were not〉 형태로 쓰며, '~이 아니었다, ~없었다'라고 해석한다.

	인칭	be동사의 과거형	부정문
단수	1인칭	I was	I was not = I wasn't
	2인칭	You were	You were not = You weren't
	3인칭	He was She was It was	He was not = He wasn't She was not = She wasn't It was not = It wasn't
복수	1인칭	We were	We were not = We weren't
	2인칭	You were	You were not = You weren't
	3인칭	They were	They were not = They weren't

ex ▶
- My sister wasn't late for school yesterday.
- They weren't famous 10 years ago.

C be동사 과거형의 의문문

〈was/were + 주어 ~?〉 형태로 쓰며, '~이었습니까?, ~있었습니까?'라고 해석한다.

긍정문	의문문	긍정 대답	부정 대답
I was	Was I ~?	Yes, you were.	No, you weren't.
You were	Were you ~?	Yes, I was.	No, I wasn't.
He was She was It was	Was he ~? Was she ~? Was it ~?	Yes, he was. Yes, she was. Yes, it was.	No, he wasn't. No, she wasn't. No, it wasn't.
We were You were They were	Were we ~? Were you ~? Were they ~?	Yes, you/we were. Yes, we were. Yes, they were.	No, you/we weren't. No, we weren't. No, they weren't.

ex ▶
- A: Was he busy last month?   B: Yes, he was.
- A: Were you in Canada last year?   B: No, I wasn't. I was in America.

Grammar Check-Up

O1 다음 중 알맞은 것을 고르시오.

1) We was | were in England last year.

2) Was | Were your brother at home last night?

3) Was | Were Karen and Chris in the library last Sunday?

2) last night 어젯밤
3) library 도서관

O2 빈칸에 알맞은 be동사의 형태를 쓰시오.

1) They _____ in the garden ten minutes ago.

2) Today the weather _____ sunny, but yesterday it
_____ rainy.

3) Ⓐ _____ you an elementary school student last year?

Ⓑ Yes, I _____.

4) Last night my father _____ in Hongkong, but he
_____ in Korea now.

1) ago ～전에
2) weather 날씨
3) elementary school
초등학교

O3 다음 문장을 지시대로 바꾸어 쓰시오.

1) Karen and Chris were at the party.

부정문 ▶ _____

2) Sue was sick yesterday.

의문문 ▶ _____

3) My friend was in New York last year.

부정문 ▶ _____

O4 다음 우리말을 영작하시오.

1) 나는 10분 전에 서울역에 있었다.

→ _____

2) 그 뮤지컬은 재미있었니?

→ _____

2) musical 뮤지컬

Unit 17 일반동사의 과거형

A 일반동사의 과거형

주로 yesterday, last, ago 등과 함께 쓰여 과거의 동작이나 상태를 나타낸다. 일반동사의 과거형은 규칙 변화와 불규칙 변화가 있다.

▶ **일반동사 과거형의 규칙 변화**

ⓐ 대부분의 동사는 동사원형에 -ed를 붙인다.	learn → learned
ⓑ -e로 끝나는 일반동사는 -d를 붙인다.	live → lived
ⓒ 〈자음 + -y〉로 끝나는 일반동사는 y를 i로 고치고 -ed를 붙인다. 〈모음 + -y〉로 끝나는 일반동사는 -ed를 붙인다.	try → tried play → played
ⓓ 〈단모음 + 단자음〉으로 끝나는 일반동사는 끝자음을 한 번 더 쓰고 -ed를 붙인다.	stop → stopped

ex • He enjoyed the party yesterday.

➕ **일반동사 과거형의 불규칙 변화**

have → had, go → went, buy → bought, teach → taught, eat → ate, meet → met

ex • I bought a loaf of bread at the bakery.　　　　　　▶ pp. 118-119의 불규칙 동사 변화표 참조

B 일반동사 과거형의 부정문

주어 + did not (=didn't) + 동사원형 (…가 ~하지 않았다)

ex • Karen studied math hard. → Karen didn't study math hard.
　　• Chris taught English to us. → Chris didn't teach English to us.

C 일반동사 과거형의 의문문

Did + 주어 + 동사원형 ~? (…가 ~했니?)

ex • A: Did Karen like the cheese cake?　　B: Yes, she did. / No, she didn't.
　　• A: Did they build the boat?　　B: Yes, they did. / No, they didn't.

Grammar Check-Up

정답 및 해설 **p.12**

Note

O1 다음 동사의 과거형을 쓰시오.

1) enjoy – _____

2) drop – _____

3) think – _____

4) cry – _____

5) speak – _____

6) eat – _____

6) teach – _____

7) meet – _____

O2 빈칸에 주어진 단어의 알맞은 형태를 쓰시오.

1) She _____ a computer a week ago. (buy)

2) They didn't _____ computer games. (play)

3) Did he _____ his hair? (wash)

4) Ted _____ Korean last year. (study)

3) wash one's hair
머리를 감다

O3 다음 문장을 지시대로 바꾸어 쓰시오.

1) She met her friends last Saturday.

부정문 _____

2) Chris and Karen lived in Korea five years ago.

부정문 _____

3) They had a nice holiday.

의문문 _____

3) holiday 휴일

O4 다음 우리말을 영작하시오.

1) 나는 어젯밤에 잠을 잘 못 잤다.

→ _____

2) 그들은 오늘 오후에 축구를 했다.

→ _____

2) this afternoon
오늘 오후

18 현재완료

A 현재완료의 의미

현재완료는 〈have/has + 과거분사 (p.p)〉의 형태이며, 과거의 한 시점부터 현재까지의 기간에 걸친 경험, 계속, 결과, 완료 등을 나타낸다.

ex • He was sick yesterday. + He is sick. → He has been sick since yesterday.
　　　　　　　　　　　　　　　　　　　　　　　(그는 어제부터 지금까지 계속 아프다.)

B 현재완료의 부정문과 의문문

> • 부정문: have/has not + 과거분사
> • 의문문: Have/Has + 주어 + 과거분사 ~?

ex • He has not finished his work yet.
　　　• A: Have you ever seen a koala?　　B: Yes, I have. / No, I haven't.

C 현재완료의 용법

경험	• 과거부터 현재까지의 경험을 표현하며, '~한 적이 있다/없다'로 해석 • 주로 ever, never, once, before 등의 단어와 함께 사용 　**ex** Have you ever been to America? (미국에 가본 적이 있니?)
계속	• 과거부터 현재까지 계속 해오고 있는 것을 표현하며, '계속 ~해오고 있다'로 해석 • 주로 for, since와 함께 사용 　**ex** My father has taught English for ten years. (나의 아버지는 10년째 영어를 가르쳐오고 있다.)
결과	• 과거의 사건이 현재에 영향을 미치는 것을 나타내며, '~해서 현재 …하다'로 해석 　**ex** He has gone to England. (그는 영국에 가고 지금 여기에 없다.)
완료	• 과거부터 어떤 일을 해오다가 방금 끝난 경우의 표현이며, '지금 막 ~했다'로 해석 • 주로 just, already, yet 등의 단어와 함께 사용 　**ex** Dick has just eaten lunch. (딕은 막 점심을 먹었다.)

D 현재완료와 과거 표현

현재완료 문장에서는 과거시제를 나타내는 부사 yesterday, ago, last night 등을 쓰지 않는다.

ex • I have met her last night. (×) → I met her last night. (○)
　　　• I have finished it an hour ago. (×) → I finished it an hour ago. (○)

⊕ 현재완료와 함께 쓰는 표현

ex • already (긍정문에서) 벌써　　　　　　　　　• yet (부정문에서) 아직도, (의문문에서) 벌써
　　　• have been to ~에 가 본 적이 있다, ~에 갔다 왔다　　• have gone to ~로 가 버렸다

Grammar Check-Up

정답 및 해설 **p.12**

Note

O1 다음 문장을 현재완료시제로 바꾸어 쓰시오.

1) He cleaned his room.

→ _____

2) I was sick in bed.

→ _____

O2 다음 문장을 지시대로 바꾸어 쓰시오.

1) They have finished their work.

의문문 ▶ _____

2) I have bought her a present.

부정문 ▶ _____

2) buy (– bought – bought)
사다

O3 다음 문장을 우리말로 해석하시오.

1) He has gone to Spain.

→ _____

2) Karen has been to Paris three times.

→ _____

3) I have worked in a hospital for two years.

→ _____

4) The singer has just left the building.

→ _____

1) go (– went – gone)
가다
3) for ~동안
4) just 방금, 막
leave (– left – left)
떠나다

O4 다음 우리말을 영작하시오.

1) 그는 벌써 도착했다.

→ _____

2) 너는 전에 플로리다(Florida)에 가 본 적 있니?

→ _____

1) arrive 도착하다

01 다음 중 동사의 과거형이 <u>잘못</u> 짝지어진 것을 고르시오.

① teach – taught   ② try – tried

③ stop – stoped   ④ live – lived

⑤ meet – met

02 빈칸에 들어갈 알맞은 것을 고르시오.

> I _____ a very good movie yesterday.

① saw   ② seen   ③ have seen

④ has seen   ⑤ is seeing

03 빈칸에 들어갈 수 <u>없는</u> 것을 고르시오.

> _____ were busy last weekend.

① Mike   ② You   ③ We

④ They   ⑤ My parents

04 밑줄 친 부분이 <u>어색한</u> 문장을 고르시오.

① I <u>broke</u> a dish last night.

② They <u>came</u> back home.

③ Chris <u>visited</u> his grandmother.

④ She <u>worked</u> last Sunday.

⑤ He <u>cleanned</u> the house.

05 대화의 빈칸에 들어갈 알맞은 것을 고르시오.

> A: Have you ever seen a kangaroo?
> B: _____.

① Yes, I do   ② No, I didn't

③ Yes, I am   ④ No, I haven't

⑤ Yes, I has

06 빈칸에 들어갈 알맞은 것을 고르시오.

> _____ Chris catch a cold yesterday?

① Has   ② Was   ③ Does

④ Did   ⑤ Have

07 대화의 빈칸에 들어갈 알맞은 것을 고르시오.

> A: Did your brother play soccer after school?
> B: Yes, _____.

① he does   ② he did   ③ he has

④ he is   ⑤ he hasn't

08 빈칸에 들어갈 알맞은 것을 고르시오.

> Mina _____ in Seoul since last year.

① lives   ② lived   ③ has lived

④ have lived   ⑤ will live

09 빈칸에 알맞은 단어를 순서대로 바르게 짝지은 것을 고르시오.

> • Today it _____ sunny.
> • It _____ sunny since yesterday.

① is – was   ② is – is   ③ is – has been

④ was – is   ⑤ is – have been

10 다음 중 올바른 문장을 고르시오.

① Did she tried her best?

② I didn't bought this in 2002.

③ Did she be a student last year?

④ My sister wasn't read *Harry Potter*.

⑤ Has she been to New York?

11 다음 중 올바른 문장을 고르시오.

① They were buy flowers.

② I've been to Japan before.

③ He has already ate breakfast.

④ Last year you and I was twelve years old.

⑤ When have you finished your homework?

12 대화의 빈칸에 들어갈 알맞은 것을 고르시오.

A: Were Cindy and Mimi at the zoo yesterday?
B: No, _____.

① she wasn't ② they aren't ③ they weren't

④ they didn't ⑤ we weren't

13 다음 중 어법상 <u>틀린</u> 문장을 고르시오.

① Has your sister done her homework?

② She's been sick since last week.

③ They have never seen a lion before.

④ She wasn't at the zoo last weekend.

⑤ Karen and Chris don't watch a movie yesterday.

14 빈칸에 들어갈 알맞은 것을 고르시오.

Sophie _____ just washed her hair.

① is   ② have   ③ has

④ does   ⑤ are

15 대화의 빈칸에 들어갈 알맞은 것을 고르시오.

A: Were you at home yesterday?
B: _____. I was in the library.

① Yes, I was   ② No, I wasn't

③ Yes, I were   ④ No, I weren't

⑤ No, I am

[16-17] 다음 두 문장을 한 문장으로 나타낼 때 빈칸에 들어갈 알맞은 말을 쓰시오.

16

She went to Taiwan. + She is not here.

→ She _____ _____ to Taiwan.

17

It was hot yesterday. + It is still hot.

→ It _____ _____ hot since yesterday.

18 우리말과 일치하도록 빈칸에 알맞은 것을 순서대로 바르게 짝지은 것을 고르시오.

• 그는 전에 프랑스에 가 본 적이 있다.
  → He _____ to France before.

• 그는 일주일 전에 프랑스에 갔다.
  → He _____ to France a week ago.

① has been – went   ② gone – went

③ has gone – has gone ④ has been – has gone

⑤ has been – has been

[19-20] 빈칸에 알맞은 단어를 순서대로 바르게 짝지은 것을 고르시오.

19

• He hasn't _____ his work.
• He didn't _____ his work.

① finish – finish   ② finished – finishes

③ finished – finish   ④ finished – finished

⑤ finish – finished

20

• I have been in Korea _____ three years.
• I have been in Korea _____ last year.
• He arrived in Korea a week _____.

① for – since – ago   ② since – for – ago

③ for – for – since   ④ for – since – for

⑤ ago – for – since

정답 및 해설 p.13

O1 다음 글의 밑줄 친 부분 중 어법상 **틀린** 것을 고르시오.

> I ① heard a new song yesterday. I ② listened to the song again and again and sang the song all day long. My mom asked me to stop singing. But I ③ found an old guitar down in the cellar. I played the guitar and ④ sing the song all night. No one in my family ⑤ could sleep well last night. Today, my mom won't give me anything to eat.

- all day long 하루 종일
- cellar 지하실
- no one 아무도 ~않다

O1 다음 표를 보고 보기처럼 질문에 알맞은 대답을 쓰시오.

in Korea	two weeks	work in a hospital	ten years
live in China	2000	clean the house	today

보기 **A** How long have you been in Korea?
B I have been in Korea for two weeks.

1) **A** When did you live in China?

   B _____

2) **A** How long have you worked in a hospital?

   B _____

3) **A** What have you already done today?

   B _____

O2 다음 우리말을 읽고 바르게 영작하시오.

캐런(Karen)은 지난 주에 한국에 도착했다. 그녀는 한국에서 일주일 동안 머무르고 있다. 그녀는 5일 전에 설악산에 갔다. 어제는 인사동을 방문했다.

_____

_____

_____

_____

- last week 지난 주
- Mt. Seorak 설악산
- Insa-dong 인사동

O2 다음 빈칸에 들어갈 말로 가장 적절한 것을 고르시오.

> I have just taken my final exams. I **A**_____ tired since last week. But I watched a movie at CGV with my classmates. It **B**_____ an exciting one. After that, I met my cousin. He bought me a book as a Christmas gift.

- final exam 기말고사
- tired 피곤한

	A		**B**
①	was	–	was
②	was	–	have been
③	have been	–	was
④	has been	–	was
⑤	have been	–	has been

Chapter 08

의문사

Chapter 미리보기

when	시간	언제	why	이유	왜
where	장소	어디에서	how	방법	어떻게
who	사람	누구	which	사물 선택	어느 것
what	사물, 사람, 직업	무엇			

No pain, no gain. 고통 없이는 얻는 것도 없다.

▶ 고생 끝에 낙이 온다

19 Who, What, Which

A Who (누구)

사람에 대해 물을 때 쓰는 의문사이다. who는 '누가', whose는 '누구의', whom은 '누구를'을 뜻한다.

ex • A: Who broke the vase?   B: Minho did.
  • A: Whom/Who do you like?   B: I like Minsu.
  • A: Whose book is this?   B: It's mine.
    (= Whose is this book?)

B What (무엇)

사람의 이름이나 직업, 사물을 물을 때 쓰는 의문사이다.

ex • A: What is her name?   B: Her name is Karen.
  • A: What does your father do?   B: He is a teacher.
    (= What is your father's job?)
  • A: What are these?   B: They are flowers.
  • A: What does he want?   B: He wants a toy car.

⊕ what + 명사

• 시간 묻기 ex A: What time is it?   B: It is 7 o'clock.
• 날짜 묻기 ex A: What is the date?   B: It's May 1.
• 요일 묻기 ex A: What day is it?   B: It is Monday.
• 색깔 묻기 ex A: What color is your dress?   B: It's pink.

C Which (어느 것)

정해진 범위에서 선택을 물을 때 쓰는 의문사이다.

ex • A: Which is stronger, a lion or a tiger?   B: A lion.

▼ ▲ ▼ ▲ ▼

Grammar Check-Up

정답 및 해설 p.13

01 빈칸에 알맞은 의문사를 쓰시오.

1) Ⓐ _____ is the date?　　Ⓑ It's March 3rd.

2) Ⓐ _____ likes Karen?　　Ⓑ John does.

3) Ⓐ _____ car is this?　　Ⓑ It's my father's.

02 다음 문장의 <u>틀린</u> 부분에 밑줄을 긋고 바르게 고쳐 쓰시오.

1) Ⓐ Who is bigger, the sun or the earth?

Ⓑ The sun is.　　　　　　　　　　(→ _____)

2) Ⓐ Whose bag is this?

Ⓑ It's Karen.　　　　　　　　　　(→ _____)

3) Ⓐ What does he do at night?

Ⓑ Yes, he watches TV.　　　　　　(→ _____)

🖉
3) at night 밤에

03 다음 문장의 밑줄 친 부분이 대답이 되도록 의문문을 쓰시오.

1) Today is <u>Friday</u>.

→ _____

2) <u>Chris</u> washed the car.

→ _____

3) John likes <u>Sujin</u>.

→ _____

04 다음 우리말을 영작하시오.

1) 너는 저녁에 뭐하니?

→ _____

2) 이 공은 누구의 것이니?

_____

🖉
1) in the evening
저녁에

Unit 19 ✿ **73**

20 Where, When, How, Why

A Where (어디에서)

장소나 위치 등을 물을 때 쓰는 의문사이다.

ex
- A: Where do you live?
- A: Where is your mom?
- A: Where is the nearest subway station?
- A: Where did you meet John?

B: I live in Mok-dong.
B: She is in the bathroom.
B: It's next to the bank.
B: I met him at the park.

B When (언제)

시간이나 날짜 등을 물을 때 쓰는 의문사이다.

ex
- A: When do you usually have lunch?
- A: When were you born?
- A: When did your sister arrive?
- A: When are you going to leave for England?

B: I have lunch at two o'clock.
B: I was born on May 5, 1989.
B: She arrived yesterday.
B: I am going to leave for England tomorrow.

C How (어떻게)

방법, 날씨, 안부 등을 물을 때 쓰는 의문사이다.

ex
- A: How does your sister go to school?
- A: How did you get there?
- A: How is the weather?
  (= What is the weather like?)
- A: How are you?
  (= How is it going?, How have you been?)
- A: How was your trip?

B: She goes to school on foot.
B: By bus.
B: It's sunny.

B: I am fine.

B: It was great.

D Why (왜)

원인이나 이유를 물을 때 쓰는 의문사이다.

ex
- A: Why do you like the dog?
- A: Why do you study English?

B: Because it's cute.
B: To get a good job.

Grammar Check-Up

정답 및 해설 p.13

Note

01 빈칸에 알맞은 의문사를 쓰시오.

1) Ⓐ _____ is my bag?　　Ⓑ It's under the bed.

2) Ⓐ _____ are you?　　Ⓑ I'm not so good.

3) Ⓐ _____ is the weather like?　　Ⓑ It's snowy.

4) Ⓐ _____ do you exercise?　　Ⓑ Because I want to lose weight.

02 다음 문장의 틀린 부분에 밑줄을 긋고 바르게 고쳐 쓰시오.

1) Ⓐ How do you go to church?

   Ⓑ By foot.　　(→ _____)

2) Ⓐ Where do you have dinner?

   Ⓑ At 7 o'clock.　　(→ _____)

3) Ⓐ When did he die?

   Ⓑ Yes, last year.　　(→ _____)

3) die 죽다

03 다음 문장의 밑줄 친 부분이 대답이 되도록 의문문을 쓰시오.

1) She goes to school <u>by subway</u>.

   → _____

2) They work <u>in a bank</u>.

   → _____

3) He was born <u>on April 1, 2002</u>.

   → _____

1) subway 지하철

04 다음 우리말을 영작하시오.

1) 너의 할머니는 어디에 사시니?

   → _____

2) 너는 아침 몇 시에 일어나니?

   → _____

A How old

나이를 물을 때 쓴다.

ex • A: How old is your father?　　　　　　B: He is 40 years old.

B How tall

키를 물을 때 쓴다.

ex • A: How tall are you?　　　　　　B: I am 150 centimeters tall.

C How much

가격을 물을 때 쓴다.

ex • A: How much is this?　　　　　　B: It's three thousand won.

D How many/much

수량을 물을 때 쓴다.

> How many + 셀 수 있는 명사, How much + 셀 수 없는 명사

ex • A: How many computers do you have?　B: I have two.
　• A: How much money do you have?　　B: Three thousand won.

E How long

길이나 기간, 걸리는 시간 등을 물을 때 쓴다.

ex • A: How long is the ruler?　　　　　B: It's 30 centimeters long.
　• A: How long does it take to go to Busan?　B: It takes an hour by plane.

F How often

회수를 물을 때 쓴다.

ex • A: How often do you wash your hair?　B: I wash my hair every day.

G How far/high

거리나 높이를 물을 때 쓴다.

ex • A: How far is it from here?　　　　B: It's two kilometers.
　• A: How high is the tree?　　　　　B: It's about ten feet high.

01 빈칸에 알맞은 의문사를 쓰시오.

1) Ⓐ _____ _____ is your sister?

Ⓑ She is 5 feet tall.

2) Ⓐ _____ _____ dogs are there in your house?

Ⓑ There are two.

3) Ⓐ _____ _____ does it take to get to your school?

Ⓑ It takes ten minutes on foot.

3) on foot 걸어서

02 다음 문장의 <u>틀린</u> 부분에 밑줄을 긋고 바르게 고쳐 쓰시오.

1) Ⓐ How tall is she?

Ⓑ She is forty years old.   (→ _____)

2) Ⓐ How long do you help him?

Ⓑ Once a week.   (→ _____)

3) Ⓐ How many cat are there?

Ⓑ There are three.   (→ _____)

2) once a week
   일주일에 한 번

03 다음 문장의 밑줄 친 부분이 대답이 되도록 의문문을 쓰시오.

1) He met Chris <u>once a week</u>.

→ _____

2) I stayed there <u>for three days</u>.

→ _____

04 다음 우리말을 영작하시오.

1) 냉장고에 우유가 얼마나 있습니까?

→ _____

2) 너의 학교는 집에서 얼마나 머니?

→ _____

1) refrigerator 냉장고

01 빈칸에 들어갈 수 <u>없는</u> 것을 고르시오.

> How much _____ is there in the refrigerator?

① water　　② milk　　③ apple
④ cheese　　⑤ bread

[02-03] 대화의 빈칸에 들어갈 알맞은 것을 고르시오.

02
A: _____ do you usually eat for breakfast?
B: I eat milk and pancakes.

① What　　② Who　　③ Whose
④ How　　⑤ Where

03
A: _____ doll is that?
B: It's my sister's.

① Who　　② Whose　　③ Whom
④ Which　　⑤ What

04 대화의 빈칸에 들어갈 수 <u>없는</u> 것을 고르시오.

A: Whose MP3 player is this?
B: It's _____.

① mine　　② his　　③ Karen's
④ her　　⑤ my brother's

05 다음 중 올바른 대화를 고르시오.

① Ⓐ When do you usually have lunch?
　Ⓑ It is twelve o'clock.
② Ⓐ How many hours do you sleep?
　Ⓑ At 7 o'clock.
③ Ⓐ How tall is he?
　Ⓑ He is 6 feet tall.
④ Ⓐ How often does she play computer games?
　Ⓑ Three hours.
⑤ Ⓐ How much money do you have?
　Ⓑ Not many.

[06-08] 대화의 빈칸에 들어갈 알맞은 것을 고르시오.

06
A: _____ do you visit your grandmother?
B: I visit my grandmother once a month.

① How soon　　② How long　　③ How tall
④ How often　　⑤ How far

07
A: _____ does it take to read this book?
B: It takes about two days.

① How often　　② How long　　③ How far
④ How old　　⑤ How much

08
A: _____ is it from here to your house?
B: It is five kilometers.

① How often　　② How long　　③ How far
④ How old　　⑤ How much

09 대화의 빈칸에 공통으로 들어갈 알맞은 말을 쓰시오.

A: _____ did you watch a movie?
B: At CGV.
A: _____ are my socks?
B: On your desk.

10 다음 중 대화가 <u>어색한</u> 것을 고르시오.

① Ⓐ What day is it?
　Ⓑ It's Saturday.
② Ⓐ How much is it?
　Ⓑ It's five thousand won.
③ Ⓐ How high is Mt. Halla?
　Ⓑ It's 1,950 meters high.
④ Ⓐ Who lives in this house?
　Ⓑ Chris does.
⑤ Ⓐ How is the weather?
　Ⓑ It's next to my house.

[11-12] 질문에 알맞은 대답을 보기에서 찾아 번호를 쓰시오.

> 보기 ① It's nine o'clock.   ② At nine o'clock.
> ③ Every day.   ④ At school.

11   What time does school start?   _____

12   Where does he play soccer?   _____

13   대화의 빈칸에 들어갈 수 <u>없는</u> 것을 고르시오.

> A: _____
> B: It's six thirty.

① What time is it?
② Do you have time?
③ What's the time?
④ Do you have the time?
⑤ What time do you have?

14   대화의 빈칸에 들어갈 수 <u>없는</u> 것을 고르시오.

> A: How does your father go to work?
> B: By _____.

① bus   ② foot   ③ subway
④ taxi   ⑤ car

15   빈칸에 들어갈 단어가 <u>다른</u> 하나를 고르시오.

① How _____ money do you have?
② How _____ friends do you have?
③ How _____ brothers and sisters do you have?
④ How _____ times do you wash your car a week?
⑤ How _____ people are there in your family?

16   대화의 빈칸에 공통으로 들어갈 알맞은 것을 고르시오.

> A: _____ size do you want?   B: Small.
> A: _____ color would you like?   B: Blue.

① What   ② How   ③ Why
④ Where   ⑤ Whose

17   밑줄 친 부분이 대답이 되도록 알맞은 의문문을 쓰시오.

> A: _____
> B: <u>Karen</u> bought this digital camera.

[18-19] 우리말과 일치하도록 빈칸에 알맞은 말을 쓰시오.

18   너는 어떻게 대구에 갔니?

→ _____ _____ you _____ to Daegu?

19   대구에 가는 데 시간이 얼마나 걸리니?

→ _____ _____ does it _____ to go to Daegu?

20   다음 중 대화가 <u>어색한</u> 것을 고르시오.

① Ⓐ What does he do for a living?
   Ⓑ He teaches English.
② Ⓐ When did you meet her?
   Ⓑ I met her last weekend.
③ Ⓐ What did you do yesterday?
   Ⓑ I played basketball with my friends.
④ Ⓐ Where is the bookstore?
   Ⓑ It's downtown.
⑤ Ⓐ What is your father doing?
   Ⓑ He washes his car every day.

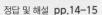
O1 대화의 밑줄 친 부분 중 어법상 틀린 것을 고르시오.

> Karen : I am home, Mom.
> Mom : ① When did school end?
> Karen : ② It was four o'clock.
> Mom : It's six o'clock now.
> ③ Why did you come home so late?
> Karen : Mom, I told you.
> Today is my friend's birthday.
> I had dinner at her house.
> Mom : ④ What did you buy for her as a birthday gift?
> Karen : ⑤ A teddy bear. It was very cute.
> She liked it very much.

O1 자연스러운 대화가 되도록 빈칸에 알맞은 질문을 쓰시오.

Ⓐ _____

Ⓑ I live in Mok-dong.

Ⓐ _____

Ⓑ I go to school on foot.

Ⓐ _____

Ⓑ I have one brother.

Ⓐ _____

Ⓑ His name is Ray.

O2 다음 빈칸에 들어갈 말로 가장 적절한 것을 고르시오.

> Chris : Do you exercise?
> Mike : Yes, I always get up early and go jogging.
> Chris : Wow.
> Mike : And then I play tennis.
> Chris : Really? Ⓐ_____ do you play tennis?
> Mike : Five times a week.
> Chris : Ⓑ_____ do you play tennis each time?
> Mike : For an hour. How about you?
> Chris : I don't exercise at all.

■ go jogging 조깅하러 가다   ■ not ~ at all 거의 ~않다

Ⓐ		Ⓑ
① How long	–	How often
② How long	–	How many
③ How often	–	How often
④ How often	–	How long
⑤ How many	–	How long

O2 다음 우리말을 읽고 바르게 영작하시오.

선생님 : 오늘은 무슨 요일이죠?
학생들 : 금요일이에요.
선생님 : 날씨가 어떻죠?
학생들 : 아주 화창해요.
선생님 : 존, 지난 주말에 뭐했니?
존 : 저는 친구들과 함께 축구를 했어요.

Teacher : _____

Students : _____

Teacher : _____

Students : _____

Teacher : _____

John : _____

Chapter 09

조동사

Chapter 미리보기

can	능력 허가 약한 추측	She can play the piano. You can use my pen. It can be true.	must	의무 강한 추측	We must (= have to) go to school. It must be true.
			should	의무	We should help elderly people.
may	허가 약한 추측	May I come in? It may be true.	will be going to	의지 미래	I will go to the library. I am going to travel to Europe.

Even a worm will turn.

▶ 지렁이도 밟으면 꿈틀한다

22 can, may

조동사의 성격	조동사 다음에는 항상 동사원형이 온다.	He can jump. (○) He can jumps. (×) He can jumped. (×)
	조동사는 동사 앞에 온다.	He can jump. (○) He jump can. (×)
	조동사의 3인칭 단수형은 없다.	He can jump. (○) He cans jump. (×)

A can

1 능력, 가능 (~할 수 있다)

> **ex** • He can run fast. = He is able to run fast.
> • My mom cannot cook Indian food. = My mom is not able to cook Indian food.

2 허가 (~해도 좋다)

> **ex** • You can use my pen.
> • A: Can I use your pen?   B: Yes, you can. / No, you can't.

3 추측 (~일 수도 있다)

> **ex** • The rumor can be true. (소문이 사실일 수도 있다.)
> • The rumor can't be true. (소문이 사실일리 없다.)

B may

1 추측 (~할/일지도 모른다)

> **ex** • She may go there. (그녀가 거기에 갈지도 모른다.)
> • She may not go there. (그녀가 거기에 안 갈지도 모른다.)

2 허가 (~해도 좋다)

> **ex** • A: May I sit here?   B: Yes, of course. / No, you may not.

⊕ can과 may의 비교

	can	may
능력	~할 수 있다 (= be able to)	×
허가	Can I ~? (~해도 될까요?)	May I ~? (~해도 될까요?)
추측	~일 수도 있다	~일지도 모른다

Grammar Check-Up

정답 및 해설 p.15

Note

O1 다음 문장의 틀린 부분에 밑줄을 긋고 바르게 고쳐 쓰시오.

1) She can swims.　　　　　　　　　　(→ _____)

2) We may can buy the book.　　　　　(→ _____)

3) Is the baby able to walks?　　　　　(→ _____)

4) He cans play the violin.　　　　　　(→ _____)

O2 다음 문장을 지시대로 바꾸어 쓰시오.

1) They can ride a bike.

　부정문 ▶ _____

2) He may be a singer.

　부정문 ▶ _____

1) ride a bike
　자전거를 타다

O3 다음 문장을 우리말로 해석하시오.

1) May I come in?

　→ _____

2) Ann may stay here.

　→ _____

3) Kate is not able to sing well.

　→ _____

2) stay 머무르다

O4 다음 우리말을 영작하시오.

1) 내일 비가 오지 않을지도 모른다.

　→ _____

2) 그들은 영어를 완벽하게 말할 수 있다.

　→ _____

1) tomorrow 내일
2) perfectly 완벽하게

23 must[have to], should

A must, have to

must	
① 의무 (~해야 한다)	② 추측 (~임에 틀림없다)
He must (= has to) go now. (그는 지금 가야 한다.)	She must be a teacher. (그녀는 선생님임에 틀림없다.)

1 must의 과거형과 미래형은 have to를 사용해서 만든다.

> ex
> • I had to leave home.
> • She will have to finish her homework.

2 must의 부정은 금지를 나타내는 must not과 불필요를 나타내는 don't have to를 사용한다.

> ex
> • He must not stay here. (그는 여기에 머무르면 절대로 안 된다.)
> • I don't have to go now. (나는 지금 갈 필요가 없다.)

Tips
• don't have to
  = don't need to
  ~할 필요가 없다

⊕ 추측을 나타내는 조동사의 비교

must	강한 추측 (~임에 틀림없다)	She must be an American. (그녀는 미국인임에 틀림없다.)
may	약한 추측 (~일지도 모른다)	She may be an American. (그녀는 미국인일지도 모른다.)
can	약한 추측 (~일 수도 있다)	She can be an American. (그녀는 미국인일 수도 있다.)

B should

should	도덕적 의무	You should keep your promises.
must (= have to)	강한 의무	You must obey the law.

> ex
> • You should study hard.
> • We should help others.
> • You should not tell a lie.

Grammar Check-Up

정답 및 해설 p.15

Note

O1 다음 문장의 틀린 부분에 밑줄을 긋고 바르게 고쳐 쓰시오.

1) He must goes to school.　　　　　　　(→ _____)

2) She has to finding the book.　　　　　(→ _____)

3) You should do not that.　　　　　　　(→ _____)

4) He don't have to know it.　　　　　　(→ _____)

🖉

2) find 찾다

O2 다음 문장을 지시대로 바꾸어 쓰시오.

1) We must do it now.

　부정문 ▸ _____

2) You should meet him.

　부정문 ▸ _____

3) We have to finish our homework today.

　부정문 ▸ _____

🖉

3) finish 끝내다

O3 다음 문장을 우리말로 해석하시오.

1) She should save some money.

→ _____

2) We must not visit there.

→ _____

3) You don't have to buy the CD.

→ _____

🖉

1) save 절약하다

O4 다음 우리말을 영작하시오.

1) 그는 그녀를 초대해야 할 것이다.

→ _____

2) 나는 일찍 일어날 필요가 없다.

→ _____

🖉

1) invite 초대하다

2) get up 일어나다

24 will, be going to

	will	be going to
기본 의미	미래 (~할 것이다)	
개별 의미	주어의 의지를 나타냄	예정이나 계획이나 예측을 나타냄

A will

1 미래

> ex • I will be at home tomorrow.
> • I will not (= won't) be at home tomorrow.
> • A: Will you visit your grandparents?   B: Yes, I will. / No, I won't.

2 주어의 의지

> ex • I will call you tomorrow. (내일 전화하겠습니다.)

• will은 '~할 것이다' 라는 미래의 뜻을 나타낼 경우 〈be going to + 동사원형〉으로 바꿀 수 있다.

B be going to

1 미래

> ex • I am going to be at home tomorrow.
> • I am not going to be at home tomorrow.
> • A: Are you going to visit your grandparents?   B: Yes, I am. / No, I am not.

2 계획된 미래

> ex • I am going to travel around Canada. (나는 캐나다를 여행할 예정이다.)

─⊕ 진행형 be going + to + 장소

be going + to + 장소 → 진행형 (~로 가고 있다)	I am going to the library now. (나는 지금 도서관에 가고 있다.)

Note

O1 다음 문장의 <u>틀린</u> 부분에 밑줄을 긋고 바르게 고쳐 쓰시오.

1) They are go to see the movie.　　　　(→ ＿＿＿＿＿＿＿)

2) We willn't stay at home.　　　　　　(→ ＿＿＿＿＿＿＿)

3) Will he passes the exam?　　　　　　(→ ＿＿＿＿＿＿＿)

O2 주어진 단어를 알맞게 배열하여 올바른 문장을 쓰시오.

1) (going, to, not, it, snow, is)

→ ＿＿＿＿＿＿＿＿＿＿＿＿＿＿＿＿＿＿＿＿＿

2) (his, sell, will, toy, he)

→ ＿＿＿＿＿＿＿＿＿＿＿＿＿＿＿＿＿＿＿＿＿

3) (him, to, she, going, meet, is, ?)

→ ＿＿＿＿＿＿＿＿＿＿＿＿＿＿＿＿＿＿＿＿＿

O3 다음 문장을 지시대로 바꾸어 쓰시오.

1) She will call him.

부정문 ＿＿＿＿＿＿＿＿＿＿＿＿＿＿＿＿＿＿＿

2) They are going to be here.

부정문 ＿＿＿＿＿＿＿＿＿＿＿＿＿＿＿＿＿＿＿

1) call 전화하다

O4 다음 우리말을 영작하시오.

1) 너는 이번 여름 방학에 무엇을 할 예정이니?

→ ＿＿＿＿＿＿＿＿＿＿＿＿＿＿＿＿＿＿＿＿＿

2) 그들은 그것을 믿지 않을 것이다.

→ ＿＿＿＿＿＿＿＿＿＿＿＿＿＿＿＿＿＿＿＿＿

2) believe 믿다

[01-03] 두 문장의 뜻이 같도록 빈칸에 알맞은 말을 쓰시오.

01
She can play the piano.

= She _____ _____ _____
play the piano.

02
I am going to give her a birthday present.

= I _____ give her a birthday present.

03
You must stop here.

= You _____ _____ stop here.

04 보기의 밑줄 친 must와 쓰임이 같은 것을 고르시오.

보기 She <u>must</u> be a teacher.

① She <u>must</u> study hard.
② They <u>must</u> get up early.
③ He <u>must</u> be happy.
④ I <u>must</u> see a dentist.
⑤ We <u>must</u> find the book.

05 밑줄 친 조동사의 의미가 다른 하나를 고르시오.

① <u>Can</u> I use your pen?
② <u>May</u> I speak to Susan?
③ <u>Can</u> you swim?
④ <u>May</u> I ask a question?
⑤ <u>Can</u> I borrow your book?

06 빈칸에 들어갈 알맞은 것을 고르시오.

David _____ the game.

① win will   ② will wins   ③ wills win
④ won't win   ⑤ will won

07 다음 중 올바른 문장을 고르시오.

① She must buys the textbook.
② He mays come here tonight.
③ They can be able to swim.
④ We don't has to buy it.
⑤ I will meet him next week.

08 다음 중 부정문이나 의문문으로의 전환이 바르지 <u>않은</u> 것을 고르시오.

① He can drive a car.
부정문► He can't drive a car.
② She has to go.
부정문► She doesn't have to go.
③ They are going to visit us.
의문문► Are going to they visit us?
④ I will go there.
부정문► I won't go there.
⑤ He had to walk home.
의문문► Did he have to walk home?

[09-11] 우리말과 일치하도록 빈칸에 알맞은 말을 쓰시오.

09
여기서 요리하면 절대 안 됩니다.

→ You _____ _____ cook here.

10
나는 책을 살 필요가 없다.

→ I _____ _____ _____ buy a
book.

11
그는 미국인일리가 없다.

→ He _____ be an American.

12 다음 문장을 미래형으로 바꿀 때 빈칸에 알맞은 말을 쓰시오.

I must leave for London.

미래형 ▶ I _____ _____ _____
leave for London.

13 빈칸에 공통으로 들어갈 알맞은 것을 고르시오.

• She _____ find the keys.
• I _____ leave now.
• We _____ not open this box.

① have
② has to
③ must
④ doesn't have to
⑤ don't have to

14 대화의 빈칸에 들어갈 알맞은 것을 고르시오.

A: Look! An old woman is carrying a heavy box.
B: We _____ help her.

① has to
② should
③ had to
④ was able to
⑤ didn't have to

15 빈칸에 들어갈 알맞은 것을 고르시오.

She _____ her friends tomorrow.

① meet
② met
③ will meet
④ had met
⑤ meeting

16 빈칸에 들어갈 알맞은 것을 고르시오.

He must _____ Jane's brother.

① is
② was
③ are
④ be
⑤ were

17 빈칸에 들어갈 수 없는 것을 고르시오.

He will _____.

① have lunch
② buys a new hat
③ play football
④ go to the library
⑤ take care of the baby

18 밑줄 친 부분이 어법상 틀린 것을 고르시오.

It is Sunday. David don't have to go to school.
①　　　　　②　　　　③　　　④　　　⑤

19 밑줄 친 부분이 어법상 틀린 것을 고르시오.

① She may come to the party.
② They are going to go fishing this weekend.
③ She can read Chinese.
④ I won't tell it to her.
⑤ He must finishes his homework.

20 두 문장의 뜻이 같지 않은 것을 고르시오.

① You don't have to park here.
= You must not park here.
② You can stay here.
= You may stay here.
③ Are they able to read English?
= Can they read English?
④ Karen doesn't have to buy those shoes.
= Karen doesn't need to buy those shoes.
⑤ She isn't going to take a piano lesson.
– She won't take a piano lesson.

정답 및 해설 **p.16**

01 다음 글의 밑줄 친 부분 중 어법상 **틀린** 것을 고르시오.

> Ann ① is going to study in Canada. We ② will miss her, but I can email ③ her. She may visit us next year. I ④ also want to study abroad. So I ⑤ must have to study English hard.

■ miss 그리워하다   ■ abroad 해외에서, 외국에서

01 다음 표를 보고 괄호 안의 우리말에 해당하는 말을 빈칸에 쓰시오.

Mon	Tue	Wed	Thur
English	Math	English	Math
Fri	Sat	Sun	
English	piano	No class	

1) I _____ study English three times a week. (~해야 한다)

2) I _____ play the piano on Saturday.
   (~할 수 있다)

3) I _____ study on Sunday.
   (~할 필요가 없다)

02 다음 괄호 안에서 어법에 맞는 표현으로 가장 적절한 것을 고르시오.

> Jane is a middle school student. She **A** (may / must) go to school during the term but she **B** (doesn't have to / have not) go to school during the vacation. She **C** (usually travels / travels usually) with her family during the vacation. This summer she will go to Canada. She wants to make some friends there.

■ during the term 학기 중에   ■ during the vacation 방학 동안

	A	**B**	**C**
①	may	– doesn't have to	– usually travels
②	may	– have not	– travels usually
③	must	– doesn't have to	– usually travels
④	must	– have not	– usually travels
⑤	must	– doesn't have to	– travels usually

02 다음 우리말을 읽고 바르게 영작하시오.

앨리스(Alice)는 영어를 잘 말한다. 나는 영어를 잘 말하지 못한다. 나는 영어를 열심히 공부해야 한다. 나는 매일 영어 일기를 쓸 것이다.

_____

_____

_____

_____

■ keep a diary 일기를 쓰다

Chapter 10

to부정사와 동명사

Chapter 미리보기

to부정사 (to + 동사원형)	명사적 용법: 주어, 목적어, 보어 역할 형용사적 용법: 명사 수식 부사적 용법: 목적, 원인 등의 의미를 나타냄	want decide plan hope } + to부정사
동명사 (동사원형-ing)	주어, 목적어, 보어, 전치사의 목적어 역할	enjoy finish give up } + 동명사

Seeing is believing.

▶ 보는 것이 믿는 것이다.

25 to부정사

A 명사적 용법

to부정사가 문장에서 주어, 목적어, 보어 역할을 한다.

1 주어 역할

ex • To sing is fun. → It is fun to sing.
　　　　　　　　　　　(가주어)　　(진주어)
　　• To meet friends is fun. → It is fun to meet friends.
　　　　　　　　　　　　　　　　(가주어)　　　　(진주어)

> 주어 자리에 있는 to부정사의 위치를 문장 뒤로 보내는 경우, 빈 주어 자리에 가주어 it을 쓴다.

2 목적어 역할

ex • I want to swim.
　　• I plan to go to London.

3 보어 역할

ex • My hobby is to swim. (my hobby = to swim)
　　• My dream is to travel around the world. (my dream = to travel)

B 형용사적 용법

to부정사가 형용사로 쓰여 명사를 뒤에서 수식한다.

ex • I have something to eat.

C 부사적 용법

to부정사가 부사로 쓰여 '목적'과 '원인' 등의 의미를 나타낸다.

1 목적

ex • We went to the library to study.
　　• I met Jane to go to the movies.

2 원인

ex • I am glad to meet you.

▼ ▲ ▼ ▲ ▼
Grammar Check-Up

정답 및 해설 p.17

O1 밑줄 친 to부정사의 용법(명사/형용사/부사)을 쓰시오.

1) She went to the shop <u>to buy</u> it.   (_____)

2) He wants <u>to watch</u> TV tonight.   (_____)

3) I don't have anything <u>to drink</u>.   (_____)

4) <u>To travel</u> to Europe is my dream.   (_____)

O2 다음 문장의 to부정사에 밑줄을 긋고, 우리말로 해석하시오.

1) They will meet Yura to get her signature.

→ _____

2) It is good for your health to exercise every day.

→ _____

1) signature 서명, 사인
2) health 건강

O3 주어진 단어를 알맞게 배열하여 문장을 완성하시오.

1) I (buy, want, to) a new bag.

→ I _____ _____ _____ a new bag.

2) I (something, do, have, to)

→ I _____ _____ _____ _____ .

3) She (study, met, to, him) English together.

→ She _____ _____ _____ _____
English together.

3) together 함께

O4 우리말과 일치하도록 to부정사를 이용하여 빈칸을 채우시오.

1) 이 상자를 드는 것은 어렵다.

→ It is difficult _____ .

2) 우리는 요리하는 것을 좋아한다.

→ We like _____ .

3) 그녀는 잠을 자기 위해 집으로 갔다.

→ She went home _____

1) lift 들어올리다
2) cook 요리하다

26 동명사

A 주어 역할

'~하는 것은'이라고 해석한다.

ex
• Swimming is fun.
• Meeting friends is fun.

B 목적어 역할

'~하는 것을'이라고 해석한다.

ex
• She enjoys dancing.
• He finished playing the piano.

⊕ to부정사/동명사를 목적어로 사용하는 동사

동사 + to부정사		동사 + 동명사	
want decide plan hope	+ to부정사	enjoy finish give up	+ 동명사
• We want to eat pizza. • I hope to meet him again. • I decided to study English grammar.		• We enjoy swimming. • I finished doing my homework. • I gave up playing games.	

C 보어 역할

'~하는 것이다'이라고 해석한다.

ex
• My hobby is singing.
• Her dream is winning the game.

D 전치사의 목적어

전치사 뒤에 동사가 올 경우 동명사를 쓴다.

ex
• Thank you for coming.
• She is good at playing the piano.

Grammar Check-Up

정답 및 해설 p.17

O1 밑줄 친 동명사의 역할(주어/목적어/보어)을 쓰시오.

1) She gave up <u>eating</u> cookies. (_____)

2) <u>Talking</u> to foreigners is interesting. (_____)

3) Thank you for <u>inviting</u> me. (_____)

4) His job is <u>taking</u> care of old people. (_____)

2) foreigner 외국인

3) invite 초대하다

O2 다음 중 알맞은 것을 고르시오.

1) Jane decided to learn | learn Korean.

2) She finished to read | reading an English book.

3) He enjoys to ride | riding his bike.

4) I want to paint | painting my best friend.

O3 다음 문장을 우리말로 해석하시오.

1) Making a movie is hard.

→ _____

2) Her hobby is riding a horse.

→ _____

3) I enjoyed watching football.

→ _____

2) ride a horse 말을 타다

O4 우리말과 일치하도록 동명사를 사용하여 빈칸을 채우시오.

1) 나는 내 방 청소를 끝냈다.

→ I _____ .

2) 나는 친구들과 수다 떠는 것을 즐긴다.

→ I enjoy _____ .

3) 액션 영화를 보는 것은 재미있다.

→ _____ is fun

2) chat 수다를 떨다

3) action movies 액션 영화

Unit 26 ♣ **95**

내신 족집게 문제

[01-03] 주어진 동사를 어법에 맞게 바꾸어 쓰시오.

01
We finished _____. (exercise)

02
He wants _____ me. (meet)

03
I have nothing _____. (eat)

[04-05] 우리말과 일치하도록 주어진 단어를 이용하여 빈칸을 채우시오.

04
그녀는 바다에서 낚시하는 것을 좋아한다.
→ She enjoys _____ in the sea. (fish)

05
나는 너를 만나서 반갑다.
→ I am glad _____ you. (meet)

06 주어진 단어를 이용하여 빈칸에 알맞을 말을 쓰시오.

A: What are they going to do this weekend?
B: They decided _____ the house. (paint)

07 빈칸에 들어갈 알맞은 것을 고르시오.

_____ English is not easy.

① Speak   ② Spoke   ③ Speaking
④ To speaking ⑤ To be spoken

08 밑줄 친 to부정사의 용법이 다른 하나를 고르시오.

① He decided to go to New York.
② She didn't want to go to the library.
③ He hopes to see her again.
④ We went to Tim's house to help him.
⑤ They like to play basketball.

09 빈칸에 알맞은 단어를 순서대로 바르게 짝지은 것을 고르시오.

· We finished _____ dinner.
· Thank you for _____ for us.

① to eat – to cook   ② to eat – cooking
③ eat – cook   ④ eating – to cook
⑤ eating – cooking

10 빈칸에 들어갈 수 없는 것을 고르시오.

He _____ to go to Lotte World.

① hopes   ② wants   ③ planned
④ enjoys   ⑤ decided

11 빈칸에 들어갈 알맞은 것을 고르시오.

We _____ singing in the contest.

① decided   ② want   ③ planned
④ finished ⑤ hope

12 빈칸에 공통으로 들어갈 말을 쓰시오.

· She planned _____ study abroad.
· I have something _____ eat.

13 우리말과 일치하도록 주어진 단어를 알맞게 배열하시오.

그녀는 영어를 공부하기 위해 MP3 플레이어를 샀다.
(bought, study, an, she, English, to, MP3 player)

→ _____

14 두 문장이 같은 뜻이 되도록 빈칸에 알맞은 말을 쓰시오.

To make good friends is not easy.

→ _____ to make good friends.

15 빈칸에 들어갈 알맞은 것을 고르시오.

I have _____ to drink.

① something　② one thing　③ anything
④ next thing　⑤ the thing

16 빈칸에 들어갈 알맞은 것을 고르시오.

We are happy _____ you.

① saw　　　② to seeing　③ seen
④ see　　　⑤ to see

17 빈칸에 들어갈 알맞은 것을 고르시오.

It is difficult _____ the questions.

① answers　② answering　③ answered
④ answer　　⑤ to answer

[18-19] 보기의 밑줄 친 to부정사와 용법이 같은 것을 고르시오.

18
보기 She went to a bookstore to buy some books.

① His hobby is to collect old books.
② She planned to climb Mt. Everest.
③ She wants to see him.
④ It is not easy to read Chinese.
⑤ They are saving some money to buy a new car.

19
보기 He wants to change his hair style.

① It is difficult to repair a bike.
② Her dream is to become a singer.
③ She decided to visit her uncle in Seattle.
④ He went to the shop to buy a pen.
⑤ His hobby is to collect stamps.

20 다음 두 문장의 뜻이 같지 않은 것을 고르시오.

① It is hard to learn English.
= Learning English is hard.
② Her job is to teach math.
= Her job is teaching math.
③ Mary likes to skate.
= Mary likes skating.
④ Karen plays the violin well.
= Karen is good at playing the violin.
⑤ She stopped to talk on the phone.
= She stopped talking on the phone.

정답 및 해설 **p.18**

O1 다음 글의 밑줄 친 부분 중 어법상 **틀린** 것을 고르시오.

> My dream is ① to become a pianist. Last year, I decided to participate in a piano contest. I hoped ② winning the contest. I practiced ③ hard to win the contest. ④ It was not easy to practice the piano every day. My mom helped me to ⑤ keep doing it. Finally, I won first prize.

- participate in ~에 참가하다
- contest 대회, 시합
- keep ~ing ~을 계속하다
- win first prize 일등상을 타다

O1 주어진 단어를 이용하여 다음 우리말을 영작하시오.

> decide   finish   give up   read   help   run

1) 그는 가난한 사람들을 돕기로 결심했다.

→ _____

2) 그녀는 뛰는 것을 포기했다.

→ _____

3) 나는 '해리 포터'를 읽는 것을 끝마쳤다.

→ _____

O2 다음 우리말을 읽고 바르게 영작하시오.

내 꿈은 외교관이 되는 것이다. 나는 외국에서 공부하기를 원한다. 나는 영어 시험에 통과하기 위해 열심히 공부한다. 영어를 공부하는 것은 쉽지 않다. 그러나 나는 나를 도와줄 사람이 있다.

_____

_____

_____

_____

_____

- diplomat 외교관
- abroad 해외에서, 외국에서

O2 다음 괄호 안에서 어법에 맞는 표현으로 가장 적절한 것을 고르시오.

> Jane and David enjoy Ⓐ(to travel / traveling). They went to China last year. They decided Ⓑ(to go / going) to London this year. They bought flight tickets to London but they had to give up Ⓒ(to fly / flying) there because David broke his leg last month.

- flight ticket 항공권
- break one's leg 다리가 부러지다

Ⓐ		Ⓑ		Ⓒ
① to travel	–	to go	–	to fly
② to travel	–	going	–	flying
③ traveling	–	to go	–	flying
④ traveling	–	going	–	flying
⑤ traveling	–	to go	–	to fly

Chapter 11

접속사

Chapter 미리보기

and (그리고), **or** (또는), **but** (그러나), **so** (그래서)	• and, or, but은 단어와 단어, 구와 구, 절과 절을 연결 • so는 절과 절만 연결
when (~할 때), **before** (~하기 전에), **after** (~한 후에), **until** (~할 때까지), **because** (~하기 때문에), **if** (만약 ~한다면)	시간이나 조건을 나타내는 부사절에서는 현재시제가 미래시제를 대신함
that (~하는 것)	that절은 문장에서 주어, 목적어, 보어 역할

Make hay while the sun shines. 햇볕이 있는 동안에 건초를 만들어라.
▶ 기회가 있을 때 잡아라.

27 and, or, but, so

A and (그리고)

• 단어 + 단어   ex▶ Colin is smart and funny.
• 구 + 구   ex▶ There are some books on the desk and under the chair.
• 절 + 절   ex▶ He ate lunch and he played basketball.

⊕ 세 단어 이상 연결할 때 접속사는 보통 마지막 단어 바로 앞에 쓴다.

ex▶ • She likes strawberries, oranges, and melons.

B or (또는)

• Which is heavier, an elephant or a rabbit?

C 명령문 + and vs. 명령문 + or

명령문 + and + 주어 + 동사 (~해라, 그러면 …한다)	Study hard, and you will pass the test. = If you study hard, you will pass the test. (열심히 공부해라, 그러면 너는 시험에 통과할 것이다.)
명령문 + or + 주어 + 동사 (~해라, 그렇지 않으면 …한다)	Study hard, or you will fail the test. = If you don't study hard, you will fail the test. (열심히 공부해라, 그렇지 않으면 너는 시험에 떨어질 것이다.)

D but (그러나)

• This building is old but beautiful.

E so (그래서)

• I woke up late, so I was late for school.

⊕ so vs. because

so → 결과	because → 이유
It looks strange, so I don't like it. 이유　　　　　결과	I don't like it because it looks strange. 결과　　　　　　이유

▽ ▲ ▽ ▲ ▽
Grammar Check-Up

정답 및 해설 p.18

01 빈칸에 and나 or 중 알맞은 접속사를 쓰시오.

1) Which color do you like better, blue _____ red?

2) He will vacuum the floor, _____ she will mop it.

3) Wake up now, _____ you will be late for school.

4) Do your best, _____ you will win the game.

2) vacuum
진공청소기로 청소하다
mop 대걸레로 닦다

02 다음 두 문장을 알맞은 접속사를 사용하여 한 문장으로 쓰시오.

1) We went shopping. + We bought some shirts.

→ _____

2) This spaghetti looks good. + It tastes bad.

→ _____

3) It is very cold outside. + I don't want to go out.

→ _____

4) You can stay here. + You can leave now.

→ _____

03 우리말과 일치하도록 빈칸에 알맞은 접속사를 쓰시오.

1) 우리는 점심을 많이 먹었기 때문에 배가 고프지 않다.

→ We aren't hungry _____ we had a big lunch.

2) 그는 어젯밤에 잠을 잘 못자서 머리가 아프다.

→ He didn't sleep well last night, _____ he had a headache.

2) headache 두통

04 다음 우리말을 영작하시오.

1) 우리는 주말에 영화를 보거나 축구하는 것을 좋아한다.

→ _____

2) 그녀는 기차를 놓쳐서 거기에 갈 수 없었다.

→ _____

2) miss 놓치다

28 when, before, after, until

A when + 주어 + 동사

'~할 때'를 뜻한다.

1 종속절, 주절 어느 것이나 먼저 나올 수 있다. 단, 종속절이 먼저 나올 경우 콤마(,)를 사용한다.

ex
- She went to Busan when she was ten. = When she was ten, she went to Busan.
  주절   종속절   종속절   주절

2 시간을 나타내는 부사절에서는 현재시제가 미래시제를 대신하므로 미래형 조동사 will을 사용하지 않는다.

ex
- I will call you when I finish my homework. (○)
- I will call you when I will finish my homework. (×)

⊕ 접속사 when vs. 의문사 when

접속사 when (~할 때)	의문사 when (언제)
When + 주어 + 동사 (평서문)	When + 동사 + 주어 ~? (의문문)
When she was a child, she was so small.	When does the movie start?

B before/after + 주어 + 동사

before는 '~하기 전에', after는 '~한 후에'를 뜻한다.

ex
- I washed my hands before I ate lunch.
  = After I washed my hands, I ate lunch.

⊕ before와 after는 접속사 뿐만 아니라 전치사로도 사용할 수 있음

접속사 (before/after) + 절 (주어+동사)	전치사 (before/after) + 명사
We had sandwiches before/after we went to school.	We had sandwiches before/after school.

C until + 주어 + 동사

'~할 때까지'를 뜻한다.

ex
- He will wait for her until she comes.

Grammar Check-Up

정답 및 해설 p.18

O1 다음 중 알맞은 것을 고르시오.

1) We lived in Seoul   after | until   we moved to Busan.

2) Mom turns off the lights   before | after   she goes out.

3) She will go out   after | until   she finishes her homework.

O2 올바른 문장이 되도록 연결하시오.

1) We played football •   • ⓐ until mom called us.

2) He found his role model •   • ⓑ before she goes to school.

3) She always has breakfast •   • ⓒ when he was 12.

O3 다음 두 문장을 주어진 접속사를 이용하여 한 문장으로 쓰시오.

1) I read a story book. + I go to bed. (before)

→ _____

2) He was shocked. + He heard the news. (when)

→ _____

O4 다음 문장을 우리말로 해석하시오.

1) When he was in New York, he played American football.

→ _____

2) When did you go to Canada?

→ _____

O5 다음 우리말을 영작하시오.

1) 나는 피곤할 때 음악을 듣는다.

→ _____

2) 나는 엄마가 집에 오기 전에 숙제를 끝낼 것이다.

→ _____

1) listen to music
음악을 듣다
2) come home 집에 오다

29 because, if, that

A because + 주어 + 동사

'~하기 때문에'를 뜻한다. because 뒤에는 원인, 이유를 나타내는 절이 나온다.

ex • I didn't go to school because I was ill.
= Because I was ill, I didn't go to school.

B if + 주어 + 동사

'만약 ~한다면'을 뜻한다.

1 종속접속사 if 뒤에는 조건을 나타내는 절이 나온다.

ex • You will pass the exam if you study hard.
= If you study hard, you will pass the exam.

2 조건을 나타내는 부사절에서는 현재시제가 미래시제를 대신하므로 미래형 조동사 will을 사용하지 않는다.

ex • She will be happy if he invites her to the party. (○)
• She will be happy if he will invite her to the party. (×)

C that + 주어 + 동사

명사절인 that절은 문장에서 주어, 목적어, 보어 역할을 한다.

1 **주어** : ~하는 것은

ex • That he won first prize is true.
= It is true that he won first prize.
　(가주어)　　　　(진주어)

2 **목적어** : ~하는 것을

ex • I know (that) he is kind.

3 **보어** : ~하는 것이다

ex • The problem is that we don't have any time.

Tips
• 목적어로 쓰인 that은 생략할 수 있다.
• that절을 목적어로 하는 동사 : know, think, believe, hope 등

⊕ 접속사 that vs. 지시대명사 that

접속사 that	지시대명사 that
I think (that) he is right.	That is my book.

Grammar Check-Up

정답 및 해설 p.18

Note

01 다음 중 알맞은 것을 고르시오.

1) If | That it is rainy tomorrow, we will stay at home.

2) We couldn't go out because | that it snowed heavily.

3) I think because | that he is a football player.

2) heavily
    (양, 정도가) 아주 많이

02 빈칸에 알맞은 접속사를 쓰시오.

1) Please call me _____ you can't come.

2) I think _____ she is clever.

3) She cried _____ she was afraid.

4) You should be hurry _____ you don't want to be late.

2) clever 영리한
3) afraid 두려운

03 다음 문장을 우리말로 해석하시오.

1) They think that he will come here.

→ _____

2) Mina could finish her homework because he helped her.

→ _____

04 다음 우리말을 영작하시오.

1) 만약 내일 일찍 일어나면 나는 운동을 할 것이다.

→ _____

2) 그녀는 늦잠을 잤기 때문에 늦었다.

→ _____

3) 그는 그녀가 의사라는 것을 안다.

→ _____

1) exercise 운동하다
2) oversleep 늦잠을 자다

내신 족집게 문제

[01 - 03] 우리말과 일치하도록 빈칸에 알맞은 것을 고르시오.

01
> 그는 아팠기 때문에 집에 가야 했다.
> → He had to go home _____ he felt sick.

① because ② before ③ that
④ if ⑤ so

02
> 밖이 추워. 코트를 가져가, 그렇지 않으면 감기에 걸릴 거야.
> → It is cold outside. Take your coat, _____ you will catch a cold.

① and ② before ③ but
④ or ⑤ after

03
> 파티에 와, 그러면 재미있게 놀 거야.
> → Come to the party, _____ you will have some fun.

① and ② before ③ but
④ or ⑤ after

[04 - 06] 우리말과 일치하도록 빈칸에 알맞은 말을 쓰시오.

04
> 만약 그가 게임에서 이긴다면 우승자가 될 것이다.
> → _____ he wins the game, he will be the champion.

05
> 그녀는 아홉 살 때 시드니에서 살았다.
> → She lived in Sydney _____ she was nine.

06
> 나는 배가 고파서 샌드위치를 만들었다.
> → I was hungry, _____ I made sandwiches.

07 밑줄 친 부분 중 가장 <u>어색한</u> 것을 고르시오.

① I want to stay at home <u>because</u> it is raining.
② He broke his leg <u>so</u> he couldn't come.
③ She likes skating <u>because</u> it is exciting.
④ He lost money <u>so</u> he couldn't buy a new cell phone.
⑤ It looks strange <u>because</u> I don't like it.

08 빈칸에 공통으로 들어갈 알맞은 말을 쓰시오.

> • She is not a painter _____ a writer.
> • I like English _____ my sister likes Chinese.

09 밑줄 친 부분 중 생략할 수 있는 것을 고르시오.

① <u>That</u> book is mine.
② She has <u>that</u> coat, too.
③ <u>That</u> man is a doctor.
④ I think <u>that</u> the computer is broken.
⑤ Look at <u>that</u> girl with long hair.

[10 - 11] 두 문장이 같은 뜻이 되도록 빈칸에 알맞은 말을 쓰시오.

10
> Exercise, and you will become healthier.
> → If _____ _____, you will become healthier.

11
> Hurry up, or you will miss the shuttle bus.
> = If _____ _____ _____ _____, you will miss the shuttle bus.

12 빈칸에 들어갈 수 <u>없는</u> 것을 고르시오.

He played the piano _____.

① after he had lunch ② after lunch
③ when lunch ④ before lunch
⑤ before he had lunch

13 다음 중 when의 쓰임이 <u>다른</u> 하나를 고르시오.

① Did you hurt yourself <u>when</u> you fell on the ice?
② <u>When</u> did you meet Tim?
③ <u>When</u> he met her, he asked her phone number.
④ He came home <u>when</u> the war was over.
⑤ <u>When</u> the movie ended, we all cried.

14 두 문장이 같은 뜻이 되도록 빈칸에 알맞은 말을 쓰시오.

Before Tim watched TV, he finished his homework.
= _____ Tim finished his homework, he watched TV.

15 빈칸에 들어갈 알맞은 것을 고르시오.

She had a free ticket, so she went to the concert.
= She went to the concert _____ she had a free ticket.

① so ② because ③ and
④ but ⑤ or

16 빈칸에 들어갈 알맞은 것을 고르시오.

He slept _____ his mom woke him up.

① or ② until ③ if
④ that ⑤ because

17 빈칸에 알맞은 단어를 순서대로 바르게 짝지은 것을 고르시오.

• We will go hiking _____ it is sunny.
• He wanted to be a policeman _____ he was a child.

① when – if ② when – so ③ because – if
④ if – when ⑤ if – that

18 빈칸에 들어갈 수 <u>없는</u> 것을 고르시오.

I _____ that she keeps her promises.

① believe ② hope ③ think
④ do ⑤ know

19 밑줄 친 부분이 어법상 틀린 것을 고르시오.

① Go now, <u>or</u> you will be late for school.
② Study hard, <u>and</u> you will pass the exam.
③ Do your best, <u>and</u> you will win the game.
④ Take an umbrella, <u>and</u> you will get wet.
⑤ Hurry up, <u>or</u> you will miss the bus.

20 다음 중 올바른 문장을 고르시오.

① I will finish cleaning the house before she will arrive.
② I will wait until he will come.
③ I will be a fire fighter when I will grow up.
④ I can't go swimming because of I have a cold.
⑤ If it rains tomorrow, we will play cards at home.

01 다음 글의 밑줄 친 부분 중 어법상 틀린 것을 고르시오.

> Ann Brown was a figure skater ① but a singer.
> She became ② a figure skater ③ when she
> was 10. She won two gold medals at the
> Olympics. She was also famous for her beauty.
> She ④ had to retire when she broke her leg.
> Then she became one of ⑤ the most popular
> singers in the world. She married another
> singer and had two sons. She died of cancer
> in 2000.

- beauty 아름다움, 미   · retire 은퇴하다
- marry 결혼하다   · die 죽다   · cancer 암

01 다음 문장을 읽고 뒷부분에 해당하는 것을 찾아 쓰시오.

1) She had two dogs _____

2) She will go to the movies _____

3) He felt much better _____

> ⓐ after he took medicine.
> ⓑ when she was a child.
> ⓒ if she finishes her homework in time.

02 다음 괄호 안에서 어법에 맞는 표현으로 가장 적절한 것을 고르시오.

> David likes Italian food **A**(so / because) he
> went to "Italia," an Italian restaurant, with
> Jane. He ordered a pasta dish and she
> ordered a salad. She had tiramisu for dessert
> **B**(so / because) she likes sweet things. The
> food was delicious. They think **C**(when /
> that) "Italia" is a good restaurant.

- dish 요리   · tiramisu 티라미수(이탈리안 케이크)
- dessert 디저트, 후식   · delicious 맛있는

	A		**B**		**C**
①	so	–	so	–	when
②	so	–	so	–	that
③	so	–	because	–	that
④	because	–	because	–	that
⑤	because	–	so	–	when

02 다음 우리말을 읽고 바르게 영작하시오.

팀(Tim)은 집에 온 후에 숙제를 했다. 그러고 나서 팀과 그의 남동생은 저녁을 먹기 전에 TV를 보았다. 그는 아침 일찍 일어나야 하기 때문에 일찍 잠자리에 들었다. 만약 내일 늦게 일어난다면 그는 학교에 늦을 것이다.

_____

_____

_____

_____

_____

- go to bed 잠자리에 들다

Chapter 12

전치사

Chapter 미리보기

시간 전치사		위치 · 장소 전치사			
at	시간 at five o'clock	on	~위에	up	~위로
on	요일 on Monday	under	~아래	down	~아래로
	날짜 on March 10th	next to	~옆에	into	~안으로
in	월 in March	behind	~뒤에	out of	~밖으로
	년 in 2007	in front of	~앞에	across	~을 가로질러
	계절 in spring	between	~사이에	along	~을 따라서

A bird in the hand is worth two in the bush. 손 안의 새 한 마리가 숲 속의 두 마리보다 가치가 있다.
▶ 내 주머니의 한 푼이 남의 돈 천냥보다 낫다.

30 시간을 나타내는 전치사

A at, on, in

at + 시간	on + 요일, 날짜	in + 년, 월, 계절
• at nine o'clock • at half past two • at lunch time	• on Monday • on January 17th • on my birthday	• in 2006 • in winter • in December
• at Christmas • at night • at noon	• on Christmas Day • on weekends • on Sunday morning	• in the morning • in the afternoon • in the evening

ex • I eat lunch at 2 o'clock in the afternoon.
   • We eat out on Friday evening.
   • He is going to visit his grandmother in the winter.

B until, since, for

until (till)	~까지	until 5 o'clock (5시까지)
since	~이래로, 이후로	since 5 o'clock (5시 이후로)
for	~동안	for 5 hours (5시간 동안)

ex • Let's wait until tomorrow.
   • My grandmother has been in hospital since last Monday.
   • She waited for me for two hours.

⊕ for, during → '~동안'의 뜻

for + 숫자		during + 기간	
• for an hour	• for three months	• during lunch time	• during vacation

ex • We stayed there for three days.
   • I will go to France during summer vacation.

Grammar Check-Up

정답 및 해설 p.20

01 빈칸에 at, on, in 중 알맞은 전치사를 쓰시오.

1) _____ a quarter past one

2) _____ 1999

3) _____ autumn

4) _____ August

5) _____ August 15th

6) _____ midnight

1) quarter 15분

3) autumn = fall 가을

02 다음 질문에 알맞은 대답이 되도록 빈칸을 채우시오.

1) A When do you visit your grandparents?

B I visit them _____ Sundays.

2) A How long have you been in Korea?

B I have been in Korea _____ ten years.

3) A How long have you known her?

B I have known her _____ last year.

2) have been in
~에 머무르고 있다

03 다음 문장을 우리말로 해석하시오.

1) I'll go snowboarding during winter vacation.

→ _____

2) I go shopping on Saturdays.

→ _____

3) We have had a lot of snow since last Saturday.

→ _____

1) go -ing ~하러 가다

04 우리말과 일치하도록 빈칸에 알맞은 말을 쓰시오.

1) 나는 매일 두 시간 동안 피아노를 친다.

→ I play the piano _____ _____

every day.

2) 나의 아버지는 밤늦게 돌아오셨다.

→ My father came back late _____ _____.

위치나 장소를 나타내는 전치사

Tips
• on
  접촉해서 위에 위치
• over
  떨어진 바로 위에 위치
• between A and B
  A와 B 사이에

A 위치나 장소를 나타내는 전치사

on over	~위에	There are some books on the desk. Some birds are flying over the tree.
under	~아래	There are socks under the desk.
next to (beside/by)	~옆에	My backpack is next to the chair.
behind	~뒤에	My school is behind the subway station.
in front of	~앞에	The bakery is in front of the bookstore.
between	~사이에	The bookstore is between a bank and a supermarket.
across from	~건너편에	The bank is across from the post office.
up	~위로	She went up the stairs.
down	~아래로	She went down the stairs.
into	~안으로	She went into the kitchen.
out of	~밖으로	She went out of the kitchen.
across	~을 가로질러	She walked across the street.
along	~을 따라서	She walked along the street.
through	~을 뚫고서	She walked through the park.
to	~로	She went to the post office.
for	~을 향해서	She left for the subway station.
from	~로부터	She went from her house to the post office.

B 그 외의 전치사

1 **with** (~와 함께, ~을 가지고)

> ex • I usually take a walk with my mom.
> • I wash my hair with soap.

2 **by** (~로)

> ex • My sister always goes to school by bus.
> • I go there by train.

3 **for** (~을 위해)

> ex • This flower is for you.
> • I bought this for you.

▼ ▲ ▼ ▲ ▼
Grammar Check-Up

O1 다음 그림을 보고 빈칸에 알맞은 전치사를 쓰시오.

There is a basket _____ the
table. Some oranges are _____
the basket. The dog is _____
_____ the table. There is a ball
_____ the table.

O2 우리말과 일치하도록 빈칸에 알맞은 말을 쓰시오.

1) 벽에 그림이 한 점 있다.

→ There is a picture _____ _____ _____.

2) 나는 어제 그와 함께 무대에서 노래를 불렀다.

→ I sang a song on the stage _____ _____ yesterday.

3) 우리는 강을 따라 걸었다.

→ We walked _____ _____ _____.

4) 그 마술사는 모자에서 새를 꺼냈다.

→ The magician took a bird _____ _____ his hat.

2) sing (– sang – sung)
노래하다

4) magician 마술사

O3 다음 우리말을 영작하시오.

1) 우리는 숟가락으로 밥을 먹는다.

→ _____

2) 그는 강을 가로질러 수영했다.

→ _____

3) 그는 팀(Tim)과 존(John) 사이에 앉아 있다.

→ _____

내신 족집게 문제

01 빈칸에 공통으로 들어갈 알맞은 것을 고르시오.

> · Chris plays games _____ an hour every day.
> · She is leaving _____ New Zealand soon.

① on   ② at   ③ for
④ until   ⑤ in

02 빈칸에 공통으로 들어갈 알맞은 것을 고르시오.

> · She goes to church _____ Sundays.
> · There is a clock _____ the wall.

① on   ② at   ③ for
④ until   ⑤ in

03 우리말과 일치하도록 빈칸에 알맞은 말을 쓰시오.

> 나는 오전 10시까지 잠을 잤다.
> → I slept _____ 10 o'clock in the morning.

04 다음 중 밑줄 친 부분이 어법상 틀린 것을 고르시오.

① School starts <u>in</u> March.
② She has lunch <u>at</u> noon.
③ She was born <u>in</u> April 1.
④ I usually eat spaghetti <u>with</u> chopsticks.
⑤ There are a lot of eggs <u>in</u> the refrigerator.

05 빈칸에 공통으로 들어갈 알맞은 것을 고르시오.

> · Someone is standing _____ the door.
> · I like to listen to the radio _____ night.

① on   ② at   ③ for
④ until   ⑤ in

[06 - 08] 다음 지도를 보고 물음에 답하시오.

06 A: Where is the bookstore?

B: It is _____ the hospital and the school.

07 A: Where's the subway station?

B: It is _____ the school.

08 A: Where is your house?

B: It is _____ _____ the post office.

09 다음 중 밑줄 친 부분이 어법상 틀린 것을 고르시오.

① My birthday is <u>in January</u>.
② She made the kite <u>with he</u>.
③ They played baseball <u>for two hours</u>.
④ It has been rainy <u>since yesterday</u>.
⑤ Karen waited for me <u>until two o'clock</u>.

10 빈칸에 들어갈 말이 다른 하나를 고르시오.

① I always watch TV _____ the evening.
② It snows a lot _____ winter.
③ I ate lunch _____ a Chinese restaurant.
④ She usually draws a picture _____ the afternoon.
⑤ I go out with my friends _____ Saturday morning.

[11-13] 대화의 빈칸에 알맞은 전치사를 보기에서 골라 쓰시오.

보기 on   in   at   since   for   by

11

A: When did the Korean War break out?

B: It broke out _____ 1950.

12

A: How long has your father been sick?

B: He has been sick _____ last year.

13

A: How does Chris go to work?

B: He goes to work _____ car.

14 보기의 밑줄 친 전치사와 같은 의미로 쓰인 것을 고르시오.

보기 She stayed in China <u>for</u> three months.

① Here is a letter <u>for</u> you.

② She made spaghetti <u>for</u> me.

③ I eat apple juice <u>for</u> breakfast.

④ I read *Harry Potter* <u>for</u> two hours.

⑤ What time does the train <u>for</u> Daegu leave?

15 다음 두 문장이 같은 뜻이 되도록 빈칸을 채우시오.

My sister walks to school.

= My sister goes to school _____ .

[16-18] 다음 그림을 보고 빈칸에 알맞은 전치사를 쓰시오.

16

Our teacher is walking _____ the street.

17

A dog is running _____ the street.

18

A boy is climbing _____ the mountain.

19 우리말과 일치하도록 빈칸에 공통으로 들어갈 알맞은 말을 쓰시오.

• 나는 극장에서 캐런과 크리스 사이에 앉았다.

→ I sat _____ Karen and Chris in the theater.

• 한강은 강남과 강북 사이를 흐른다.

→ The Han River runs _____ Gangnam and Gangbuk.

20 다음 두 문장이 같은 뜻이 되도록 빈칸을 채우시오.

Karen goes for a walk every Sunday.

= Karen goes for a walk _____ Sundays.

정답 및 해설 **p.21**

01 다음 빈칸에 들어갈 알맞은 전치사를 바르게 연결한 것을 고르시오.

> I went shopping at Shinsegae department store **A**_____ my mom. She bought shoes for my dad and I bought Christmas cards. We stayed there **B**_____ an hour. Afterwards, we watched a movie in the theater near the department store. My mom and I had a good time.

■ afterwards 그 뒤에　　■ theater 극장

	A		**B**			**A**		**B**
①	on	–	for		②	with	–	for
③	with	–	since		④	to	–	until
⑤	on	–	for					

02 다음 괄호 안에서 어법에 맞는 표현으로 가장 적절한 것을 고르시오.

> I am a student in middle school. I am **A**(in / on) the first grade. I have a part-time job as a delivery boy. Every day I get up at 4:30 in the morning. I deliver newspapers from 5:00 **B**(until / for) 6:00 in the morning. It is very hard for me to get up early. But I like this job because I can exercise and make money. Also, this job gives me good experience because I want **C**(being / to be) a businessman.

■ part-time job 시간제 일　　■ delivery boy 신문배달 소년
■ experience 경험　　■ businessman 사업가

	A		**B**		**C**
①	in	–	until	–	to be
②	in	–	for	–	to be
③	on	–	until	–	being
④	on	–	until	–	to be
⑤	on	–	for	–	being

01 다음 그림을 보고 문장을 완성하시오.

탁자 위에 많은 종류의 과일들이 있다. 사과는 배와 오렌지 사이에 있다. 수박은 바나나 뒤에 있다. 복숭아는 사과 앞에 있다. 사과 위에 벌 한 마리가 있다.

There are many kinds of fruit on the table. The apple is _____ the pear _____ the orange. The watermelon is _____ a bunch of bananas. The peach is _____ _____ _____ the apple. A bee is _____ the apple.

02 다음 우리말을 읽고 바르게 영작하시오.

일요일이다. 나는 일요일에 10시까지 잠을 잔다. 나는 11시에 아침 겸 점심을 먹는다. 나는 한 시간 동안 음악을 듣는다. 나는 3시부터 5시까지 숙제를 한다. 나의 가족은 보통 6시경에 외식을 하고 영화를 본다.

_____

_____

_____

_____

_____

■ brunch 아침 겸 점심

불규칙
동사 변화표

불규칙 동사 변화표

현재	과거	과거분사
be 이다, 있다	was, were	been
become 되다	became	become
begin 시작하다	began	begun
break 깨다	broke	broken
bring 가지고 오다	brought	brought
buy 사다	bought	bought
catch 잡다	caught	caught
come 오다	came	come
cut 자르다	cut	cut
do 하다	did	done
drink 마시다	drank	drunk
drive 운전하다	drove	driven
eat 먹다	ate	eaten
fall 떨어지다	fell	fallen
find 찾다	found	found
fly 날다	flew	flown
forget 잊다	forgot	forgotten
get 얻다	got	got(gotten)
give 주다	gave	given
have 가지고 있다	had	had

현재	과거	과거분사
hear 듣다	heard	heard
know 알다	knew	known
leave 떠나다	left	left
lose 잃어버리다	lost	lost
make 만들다	made	made
meet 만나다	met	met
pay 지불하다	paid	paid
put 놓다	put	put
say 말하다	said	said
see 보다	saw	seen
sell 팔다	sold	sold
sit 앉다	sat	sat
sleep 잠자다	slept	slept
teach 가르치다	taught	taught
tell 말하다	told	told
stand 서있다	stood	stood
take 데리고 가다	took	taken
speak 말하다	spoke	spoken
think 생각하다	thought	thought
win 이기다	won	won

다음 동사의 과거형과 과거분사형을 써보세요.

현재	과거	과거분사
be 이다, 있다		
become 되다		
begin 시작하다		
break 깨다		
bring 가지고 오다		
buy 사다		
catch 잡다		
come 오다		
cut 자르다		
do 하다		
drink 마시다		
drive 운전하다		
eat 먹다		
fall 떨어지다		
find 찾다		
fly 날다		
forget 잊다		
get 얻다		
give 주다		
have 가지고 있다		

현재	과거	과거분사
hear 듣다		
know 알다		
leave 떠나다		
lose 잃어버리다		
make 만들다		
meet 만나다		
pay 지불하다		
put 놓다		
say 말하다		
see 보다		
sell 팔다		
sit 앉다		
sleep 잠자다		
teach 가르치다		
tell 말하다		
stand 서있다		
take 데리고 가다		
speak 말하다		
think 생각하다		
win 이기다		

꽉! 잡은 중학 영문법

1
Book

GRAMMAR
CATCH

저자 김명이 · 이재림

초판 1쇄 발행 2007년 5월 1일
개정판 1쇄 발행 2015년 6월 10일
개정판 5쇄 발행 2023년 6월 21일

편집장 조미자
책임편집 권민정 · 김미경 · 정진희 · 최수경
표지디자인 김교빈
디자인 김교빈 · 임미영
관리 이성희 · 신세영 · 신시아
인쇄 북토리

펴낸이 정규도

펴낸곳 Happy House

주소 경기도 파주시 문발로 211 다락원 빌딩
전화 02-736-2031 (내선 250)
팩스 02-732-2037
출판등록 1977년 9월 16일 제406-2008-000007호

Copyright ⓒ 2015, 김명이 · 이재림

ISBN 978-89-6653-187-5 53740

[Grammar Catch] 시리즈는 [오! 마이 그래머] 시리즈의 개정 증보판입니다.
정답 및 해설 무료 다운로드 www.ihappyhouse.co.kr
*Happy House는 다락원의 임프린트입니다.

꼭! 잡은 중학 영문법

GRAMMAR CATCH

★ Workbook ★

Happy House

꼭! 잡은 중학 영문법
GRAMMAR CATCH
★ Workbook ★

1 Book

Contents

Happy House

01 다음 중 알맞은 것을 고르시오.

1) My parents are | is in Jejudo.

2) I are | am 10 years old.

3) France is | are in Europe.

4) You and he is | are not tall.

5) Are | Is your mother a teacher?

6) Are | Is your books in your bag?

02 우리말과 일치하도록 빈칸에 알맞은 말을 쓰시오.

1) 너와 나는 자매이다.

→ You and I _____ sisters.

2) 내 양말은 침대 아래에 없다.

→ My socks _____ under the bed.

3) 나의 아버지는 집에 없다.

→ My father _____ at home.

4) 몇 마리의 새들이 우리 앞에 있다.

→ Some birds _____ in front of us.

5) 나는 배고프지 않다.

→ I _____ hungry.

6) 너의 할머니는 방에 계시니?

→ _____ your grandmother in her room?

03 다음 문장을 지시대로 바꾸어 쓰시오.

1) We're good neighbors.

부정문 _____

2) The magazine is boring.

부정문 _____

3) He's from Turkey.

의문문 _____

4) John and Ann are her best friends.

의문문 _____

04 밑줄 친 부분을 줄임말로 쓰시오.

1) <u>It is</u> very long.　　　　　(→ ＿＿＿＿＿＿＿)

2) <u>They are</u> often late for school.　(→ ＿＿＿＿＿＿＿)

3) <u>I am</u> from New Zealand.　　(→ ＿＿＿＿＿＿＿)

4) Kate <u>is not</u> busy now.　　(→ ＿＿＿＿＿＿＿)

5) The soldiers <u>are not</u> tall.　(→ ＿＿＿＿＿＿＿)

05 다음 질문에 대한 대답을 완성하시오.

1) Ⓐ Are you a middle school student?　Ⓑ Yes, ＿＿＿＿ ＿＿＿＿.

2) Ⓐ Are you close friends?　Ⓑ Yes, ＿＿＿＿ ＿＿＿＿.

3) Ⓐ Is your grandmother in Seoul?　Ⓑ ＿＿＿＿, ＿＿＿＿ ＿＿＿＿. She is in Sokcho.

4) Ⓐ Is the parking lot empty?　Ⓑ No, ＿＿＿＿ ＿＿＿＿.

5) Ⓐ Are her brothers kind to her?　Ⓑ Yes, ＿＿＿＿ ＿＿＿＿.

06 다음 우리말을 영어로 표현할 때 틀린 부분에 밑줄을 긋고 바르게 고쳐 쓰시오.

1) 나는 고등학생이 아니다.

I amn't a high school student.　(→ ＿＿＿＿＿＿＿)

2) 그녀의 양손은 차지 않다.

Her hands isn't cold.　(→ ＿＿＿＿＿＿＿)

3) 너의 컴퓨터는 책상 위에 있니?

Are your computer on the desk?　(→ ＿＿＿＿＿＿＿)

4) 너와 소미는 친절하다.

You and Somi is kind.　(→ ＿＿＿＿＿＿＿)

5) Ⓐ 잭슨 여사는 집에 있니? Ⓑ 아니, 없어.

Ⓐ Is Ms. Jackson at home? Ⓑ No, she is.　(→ ＿＿＿＿＿＿＿)

07 주어진 말을 이용하여 다음 우리말을 영작하시오.

1) 내 신발은 더럽지 않다. (shoes, dirty)

→ ＿＿＿＿＿＿＿

2) 그 영어책은 어렵니? (difficult)

→ ＿＿＿＿＿＿＿

3) 그들은 한국에 없다. (Korea)

→ ＿＿＿＿＿＿＿

4) 제인(Jane)과 에릭(Eric)은 나의 새로운 친구들이다. (new)

→ ＿＿＿＿＿＿＿

O1 다음 표를 보고 빈칸에 들어갈 알맞은 말을 쓰시오.

주격	소유격	목적격	소유대명사
I	my	me	1)
you	2)	you	3)
he	his	4)	his
she	her	her	5)
it	6)	it	—
we	our	7)	ours
they	8)	them	9)

O2 우리말과 일치하도록 빈칸에 알맞은 말을 쓰시오.

1) 그의 자전거는 빠르다.

→ ＿＿＿＿＿＿＿＿ bike is fast.

2) 그들은 독일 출신이다.

→ ＿＿＿＿＿＿＿＿ are from Germany.

3) 그녀는 항상 우리를 돕는다.

→ ＿＿＿＿＿＿＿＿ always helps ＿＿＿＿＿＿＿＿.

4) 저 신발들은 그들의 것이다.

→ Those shoes are ＿＿＿＿＿＿＿＿.

5) 그녀의 남동생은 이탈리아에 있다.

→ ＿＿＿＿＿＿＿＿ brother is in Italy.

6) 우리는 그를 잘 안다.

→ ＿＿＿＿＿＿＿＿ know ＿＿＿＿＿＿＿＿ well.

7) 그는 차를 한 대 가지고 있다. 그것의 색깔은 파란색이다.

→ ＿＿＿＿＿＿＿＿ has a car. ＿＿＿＿＿＿＿＿ color is blue.

O3 다음 문장의 틀린 부분에 밑줄을 긋고 바르게 고쳐 쓰시오.

1) Is you friend in her house?　　　　(→ ＿＿＿＿＿＿＿＿)

2) She has a house. It's windows are big.　　(→ ＿＿＿＿＿＿＿＿)

3) Those are not ours. They are their.　　(→ ＿＿＿＿＿＿＿＿)

4) Your friends are helping our.　　　(→ ＿＿＿＿＿＿＿＿)

5) This is your and that is mine.　　　(→ ＿＿＿＿＿＿＿＿)

6) She mother is our teacher.　　　　(→ ＿＿＿＿＿＿＿＿)

04 밑줄 친 부분을 알맞은 인칭대명사로 바꾸시오.

1) <u>Jimin and I</u> are close friends. (→ _____)
2) <u>The books</u> are in the box. (→ _____)
3) I love <u>my father</u> very much. (→ _____)
4) <u>You and James</u> are roommates. (→ _____)
5) We often visit <u>Mr. and Mrs. Johnson</u>. (→ _____)

05 두 문장이 같은 뜻이 되도록 빈칸에 알맞은 말을 쓰시오.

1) That is my guitar. = That guitar is _____.
2) These are their cars. = These cars are _____.
3) This cellphone is hers. = This is _____ cellphone.
4) Those backpacks are ours. = Those are _____ backpacks.

06 밑줄 친 부분을 알맞은 인칭대명사로 바꾸어 문장을 완성하시오.

1) I know <u>the girl</u>. Do you know _____?
2) Ⓐ Who is <u>that man</u>? Ⓑ _____ is my uncle.
3) I like <u>those boys</u>. I often play soccer with _____.
4) I have <u>a puppy</u>. _____ name is Zzong.
5) I have <u>two foreign friends</u>. _____ come from Germany.
6) <u>Kevin and I</u> are classmates. _____ both have a cute sister.

07 주어진 말을 이용하여 다음 우리말을 영작하시오.

1) 그녀는 그의 이름을 기억한다. (remember)
   → _____

2) 그는 너의 새로운 수학 선생님이니? (math)
   → _____

3) 우리는 매주 일요일 그들을 방문한다. (visit, every Sunday)
   → _____

4) 그들은 방과 후에 그들의 친구들과 함께 농구를 한다. (play basketball, after school)
   → _____

5) 제인(Jane)은 매일 그녀의 방을 청소한다. (clean, every day)
   → _____

6) 이 양말은 그들의 것이다. (these socks)
   → _____

01 다음 중 알맞은 것을 고르시오.

1) She wash | washes | washs her hair every day.

2) They go | goes | going to bed late.

3) My sister always eat | eats | eating bread for breakfast.

4) We wear | wears | wearing school uniforms at school every day.

5) Mr. Johnson have | has | haves a lot of books in his room.

6) You know | knows | knowing a lot of stories about ghosts.

7) It often rain | rains | rainy in summer.

02 우리말과 일치하도록 빈칸에 알맞은 말을 쓰시오.

1) 나의 이모는 종종 우리를 위해 떡을 만들어 주신다.
→ My aunt often _____ rice cakes for us.

2) 이 서점은 오후 11시에 문을 닫는다.
→ This bookstore _____ at 11 p.m.

3) 많은 외국인들이 매년 한국을 방문한다.
→ Many foreigners _____ Korea every year.

4) 브라운 여사는 매일 물 7잔을 마신다.
→ Mrs. Brown _____ seven glasses of water every day.

5) 그녀의 아들 진수는 저녁 식사 후에 숙제를 한다.
→ Her son Jinsu _____ his homework after dinner.

6) 그들은 매일 학교에 걸어서 간다.
→ They _____ to school every day.

7) 나는 당신의 도움이 필요하다.
→ I _____ your help.

03 주어진 동사의 현재형을 알맞게 쓰시오.

1) This math class _____ at 9. (begin)

2) My brother _____ this medicine three times a day. (take)

3) My friend Sujin _____ English hard. (study)

4) My parents _____ movies every Friday night. (watch)

5) She _____ her plants once a week. (water)

6) My mother _____ my hair every morning. (brush)

04 다음 우리말을 영어로 표현할 때 <u>틀린</u> 부분에 밑줄을 긋고 바르게 고쳐 쓰시오.

1) 그는 매일 최선을 다한다.

→ He trys his best every day. (→ _____)

2) 나의 강아지는 너무 많이 먹는다.

→ My puppy eat too much. (→ _____)

3) 지원이는 방과 후에 항상 컴퓨터 게임을 한다.

→ Jiwon always plaies computer games after school. (→ _____)

4) 그녀와 그는 화요일마다 늦게까지 일한다.

→ She and he works late every Tuesday. (→ _____)

5) 나의 조부모님은 제주도에 사신다.

→ My grandparents lives in Jejudo. (→ _____)

6) 제니는 매일 피아노 레슨을 받는다.

→ Jenny is taking a piano lesson every day. (→ _____)

05 밑줄 친 부분을 괄호 안의 단어로 바꾸어 문장을 다시 쓰시오.

1) <u>Sumi and I</u> always have noodles for lunch. (Sumi)

→ _____

2) <u>We</u> go to the museum every weekend. (He)

→ _____

06 주어진 말을 이용하여 다음 우리말을 영작하시오.

1) 우리는 아침 10시에 가게를 연다. (in the morning)

→ _____

2) 그 고양이는 매일 밤 밖으로 나간다. (every night)

→ _____

3) 나의 아버지는 일요일마다 자전거를 타신다. (ride a bike, every Sunday)

→ _____

4) 그는 3명의 친한 친구가 있다. (close)

→ _____

5) 이 식물은 빨리 자란다. (plant, grow)

→ _____

6) 그녀는 항상 식사 전에 손을 씻는다. (before meals)

→ _____

Unit 04 ▶ 일반동사의 부정문과 의문문

01 다음 중 알맞은 것을 고르시오.

1) Mr. Baker is | does not work late on Friday.

2) She doesn't cooks | cook well.

3) Do | Does they play soccer after school?

4) Does Mary has | have long hair?

5) Do | Does the baby sleep well?

6) The students don't | doesn't look happy.

02 우리말과 일치하도록 빈칸에 알맞은 말을 쓰시오.

1) 그 아이들은 매일 우유 한 잔을 마시니?

→ _____ the children _____ a glass of milk every day?

2) 이 미술관은 일요일에는 문을 열지 않는다.

→ This art gallery _____ _____ on Sunday.

3) 그는 영문법을 일주일에 두 번 공부하니?

→ _____ he _____ English grammar twice a week?

4) 그녀의 딸은 숙제를 하지 않는다.

→ Her daughter _____ _____ her homework.

03 다음 문장을 지시대로 바꾸어 쓰시오.

1) I go to bed at 9.

부정문 ▶ _____

2) They like Chinese food.

부정문 ▶ _____

3) My father does the dishes.

부정문 ▶ _____

4) He plays the drums on Friday.

의문문 ▶ _____

5) The kids read books after dinner.

의문문 ▶ _____

6) It rains there in winter.

의문문 ▶ _____

04 다음 질문에 대한 대답을 완성하시오.

1) Ⓐ Do you speak English? Ⓑ Yes, _____ _____.

2) Ⓐ Does Mr. Kim teach math? Ⓑ _____, _____ _____. He teaches Spanish.

3) Ⓐ Do your brothers like skiing? Ⓑ Yes, _____ _____.

4) Ⓐ Does she live in Seoul? Ⓑ _____, _____ _____. She lives in Busan.

5) Ⓐ Do turtles run fast? Ⓑ No, _____ _____.

05 다음 우리말을 영어로 표현할 때 틀린 부분에 밑줄을 긋고 바르게 고쳐 쓰시오.

1) 그들은 일주일에 두 번 스페인어 수업을 듣니?

Are they take Spanish lessons twice a week? (→ _____)

2) 존슨 부부는 딸이 없다.

Mr. and Mrs. Johnson doesn't have a daughter. (→ _____)

3) 그녀는 내 이름을 모른다.

She does not knows my name. (→ _____)

4) 너의 아버지는 운전을 하시니?

Do your father drive? (→ _____)

5) 너의 남동생들은 주말에 운동을 하니?

Does your brothers exercise on weekends? (→ _____)

6) 그는 매일 커피를 마시지는 않는다.

He isn't drinking coffee every day. (→ _____)

06 주어진 말을 이용하여 다음 우리말을 영작하시오.

1) 호주는 12월에 눈이 오지 않는다. (it, Australia, December)

→ _____

2) 그녀는 매운 음식을 좋아하니? (spicy food)

→ _____

3) 너의 어머니는 아침에 일찍 일어나시니? (get up, early)

→ _____

4) 너는 매일 샤워를 하니? (take a shower)

→ _____

5) 나는 아침으로 시리얼을 먹지 않는다. (cereal, breakfast)

→ _____

O1 다음 동사를 '동사원형-ing' 형태로 바꾸시오.

1) study – _____   2) come – _____

3) swim – _____   4) leave – _____

5) drop – _____   6) lie – _____

7) sing – _____   8) ski – _____

O2 우리말과 일치하도록 주어진 동사를 알맞은 형태로 쓰시오.

1) 나의 사촌은 지금 드럼을 치고 있다. (play)

→ My cousin _____ _____ the drum now.

2) 우리는 산책을 하고 있지 않다. (take)

→ We _____ _____ a walk.

3) 그들은 지금 아이스크림을 먹고 있다. (have)

→ They _____ _____ ice cream at the moment.

4) 그녀는 지금 우리를 기다리고 있습니까? (wait)

→ _____ she _____ for us now?

O3 다음 문장을 현재진행형으로 바꾸어 쓰시오.

1) My friend Karen swims every day.

→ _____ now.

2) They play baseball after school.

→ _____ at the moment.

3) Does he study English?

→ _____ now?

O4 다음 문장을 지시대로 바꾸어 쓰시오.

1) She is chatting to her friends.

부정문 ▶ _____

2) John and Ann are talking on the phone.

의문문 ▶ _____

3) I am watering plants.

부정문 ▶ _____

05 다음 질문에 대한 대답을 완성하시오.

1) Ⓐ Is your brother listening to music? Ⓑ Yes, _____ _____.

2) Ⓐ Is Mrs. Kim cooking dinner? Ⓑ _____, _____ _____. She is eating dinner.

3) Ⓐ Are the students taking an exam? Ⓑ Yes, _____ _____.

06 주어진 말을 이용하여 질문에 알맞은 대답을 쓰시오.

1) Ⓐ What are you doing now?

Ⓑ _____ (have lunch)

2) Ⓐ What is your father doing?

Ⓑ _____ (wash his car)

3) Ⓐ What are your friends doing?

Ⓑ _____ (play soccer)

07 다음 문장의 틀린 부분에 밑줄을 긋고 바르게 고쳐 쓰시오.

1) I am having a lot of toy cars. (→ _____)

2) She is eatting strawberries for dessert now. (→ _____)

3) Is your father drives a car now? (→ _____)

4) Somi and I taking a picture at the moment. (→ _____)

5) He is not learn French now. (→ _____)

6) Ⓐ Are they cleaning the house now? Ⓑ No, they don't. (→ _____)

08 주어진 말을 이용하여 다음 우리말을 영작하시오.

1) 그녀는 그녀의 가방을 찾고 있다. (look for)

→ _____

2) 브라이언(Brian)은 손을 씻고 있다. (wash his hands)

→ _____

3) 네 여동생은 지금 자고 있니? (sleep)

→ _____

4) 그들은 그 영화에 관해서 이야기하고 있지 않다. (talk about)

→ _____

5) 나의 어머니는 지금 생일 케이크를 자르고 있다. (cut, birthday cake)

→ _____

6) 그 기차는 지금 대구를 향해서 떠나가고 있다. (leave for Daegu)

→ _____

01 주어진 단어를 알맞은 형태로 바꾸어 쓰시오.

1) There are two _____ on the table. (knife)

2) There are a lot of _____ in the world. (city)

3) We have eight _____. (pear)

4) Three _____ are playing basketball. (boy)

5) I ate two _____ for breakfast. (potato)

6) There are ten _____ in the fish bowl. (fish)

7) We need four _____. (box)

8) Three _____ are sitting on the bench. (man)

02 다음 문장의 밑줄 친 부분을 바르게 고쳐 쓰시오.

1) Tom and Jane have three child.   (→ _____)

2) Kevin is cleaning two car.   (→ _____)

3) They are playing with a lot of toy.   (→ _____)

4) A lot of leaf turn red in autumn.   (→ _____)

5) Several sheep are in the field.   (→ _____)

6) The baby has two tooth.   (→ _____)

7) There are two church in my town.   (→ _____)

8) Three bus are at the bus stop.   (→ _____)

03 우리말과 일치하도록 보기의 표현을 이용하여 문장을 완성하시오.

| 보기 | a loaf of | a glass of | a piece of | a bottle of | a pair of |

1) 수지는 하루에 우유를 두 잔 마신다.
   → Suzie drinks _____ milk a day.

2) 빵 열 덩어리가 오븐 안에 있다.
   → There are _____ bread in the oven.

3) 그는 와인 한 병을 들고 있다.
   → He is holding _____ wine.

4) 제임스는 청바지 일곱 벌을 가지고 있다.
   → James has _____ jeans.

5) 우리는 종이 열 장이 필요하다.
   → We need _____ paper.

04 주어진 단어를 이용하여 단수형 문장을 복수형 문장으로 바꾸어 쓰시오.

1) There is a mouse over there. (five)

→ _____

2) Judy drinks a cup of tea every day. (two)

→ _____

3) Kate needs a pair of gloves. (four)

→ _____

4) A woman is waiting at the bus stop. (six)

→ _____

5) I have a piano at home. (two)

→ _____

05 우리말과 일치하도록 주어진 단어를 이용하여 문장을 완성하시오.

1) 케빈의 친구들은 친절하다. (Kevin, friends)

→ _____ are kind.

2) 나의 이모는 어린이책을 쓴다. (children, books)

→ My aunt writes _____.

3) 나는 그 책의 제목을 모른다. (the book, the title)

→ I don't know _____.

4) 도시 중심가에 한 여학교가 있다. (girls, school)

→ There is a _____ in the city center.

06 주어진 말을 이용하여 다음 우리말을 영작하시오.

1) 나는 후식으로 케이크 한 조각과 오렌지 주스 한 잔을 원한다. (for dessert)

→ _____

2) 세 명의 학생들이 운동장에서 놀고 있다. (playground)

→ _____

3) 그녀는 아침에 커피 한 잔을 마신다. (drink)

→ _____

4) 늑대 세 마리가 들판에서 달리고 있다. (in the field)

→ _____

O1 빈칸에 a나 an 중 알맞은 것을 쓰시오.

1) Kate eats _____ orange every day.

2) Suzie has _____ house.

3) Susan needs _____ umbrella.

4) John is drawing _____ painting.

5) This is _____ elephant.

6) Kevin studies English twice _____ week.

7) Amy rides _____ skateboard.

8) There is _____ apple on the table.

9) Jane is _____ fashion designer.

10) James is writing _____ email.

O2 다음 문장의 <u>틀린</u> 부분에 밑줄을 긋고 바르게 고쳐 쓰시오.

1) There is an university near here.　　(→ _____)

2) Harry teaches math five times the week.　(→ _____)

3) Suzie plays a piano.　　(→ _____)

4) Susan has a dinner at seven.　　(→ _____)

5) We are looking at a sky.　　(→ _____)

6) Kate goes to school by the train.　　(→ _____)

7) Paul has a car. A car is yellow.　　(→ _____)

8) It is cold here. Close door, please.　　(→ _____)

O3 다음 빈칸에 a나 an, 또는 the 중 알맞은 것을 쓰시오. 관사가 필요 없는 경우 × 표시하시오.

1) This is _____ game. _____ game is interesting.

2) They play _____ football well.

3) _____ sun rises in _____ east.

4) Suzie always has _____ breakfast.

5) Harry plays _____ cello after school.

6) Susan is _____ opera singer.

7) Turn on _____ light, please.

8) Kate goes to the hospital by _____ taxi.

9) Amy studies Chinese twice _____ week.

10) It is raining. Jane needs _____ raincoat.

O4 우리말과 일치하도록 주어진 단어를 이용하여 문장을 완성하시오.

1) 수잔은 하루에 두 번 세수한다. (day)

→ Susan washes her face twice _____.

2) 해는 서쪽으로 진다. (sun)

→ _____ sets in the west.

3) 존은 자동차를 타고 출근한다. (car)

→ John goes to work _____.

4) 창문을 열어주십시오. (window)

→ Open _____, please.

5) 폴은 한 시간 동안 영어를 공부한다. (hour)

→ Paul studies English for _____.

6) 나는 책을 한 권 가지고 있다. 그 책은 재미있다. (book)

→ I have a book. _____ is funny.

O5 우리말과 일치하도록 주어진 단어를 알맞게 배열하시오.

1) 에이미는 버스를 타고 학교에 간다. (bus, goes, by, school, to, Amy)

→ _____

2) 그녀는 아침을 먹지 않는다. (does, breakfast, she, not, eat)

→ _____

3) 내 남동생은 배드민턴을 잘 친다. (plays, badminton, brother, my, well)

→ _____

4) 그들은 바다에서 수영하고 있다. (the, swimming, are, in, sea, they)

→ _____

O6 주어진 말을 이용하여 다음 우리말을 영작하시오.

1) 지구는 둥글다. (round)

→ _____

2) 그는 한 달에 네 번 그 건물을 청소한다. (four times)

→ _____

3) 제임스(James)는 정직한 소년이다. (honest)

→ _____

4) 나의 삼촌은 일요일에 바이올린을 연주한다. (violin, on Sunday)

→ _____

01 밑줄 친 부분에 유의하여 빈칸에 알맞은 재귀대명사를 쓰시오.

1) <u>Amy</u> bakes a cake _____ .

2) <u>I</u> wrote an English book _____ .

3) <u>Harry</u> makes a sandwich _____ .

4) Let <u>me</u> introduce _____ .

5) <u>Kate and I</u> enjoyed _____ at the party.

02 알맞은 지시대명사를 이용하여 다음 질문에 대한 대답을 완성하시오.

1) **A** Is this a house?   **B** Yes, _____ _____ .

2) **A** Is that a car?   **B** No, _____ _____ .

3) **A** Are these your shoes?   **B** Yes, _____ _____ .

4) **A** Are those her pants?   **B** No, _____ _____ .

03 다음 우리말을 영어로 표현할 때 틀린 부분에 밑줄을 긋고 바르게 고쳐 쓰시오.

1) 저것들은 그녀의 책들이다.

That are her books.   (→ _____)

2) 이 사람들은 영웅들이다.

This people are heroes.   (→ _____)

3) 아홉 시다.

This is nine.   (→ _____)

4) 앤과 나는 직접 집을 장식한다.

Ann and I decorate the house herself.   (→ _____)

04 다음 문장을 우리말로 해석하시오.

1) It is Sunday.

→ _____

2) I'm eating a cheeseburger. It is my favorite food.

→ _____

3) It is windy.

→ _____

4) There is a tennis ball on the table. It is hers.

→ _____

05 빈칸에 알맞은 대명사를 쓰시오.

1) 나는 코트를 하나 가지고 있다. 그것은 멋지다.

→ I have a coat. _____ is nice.

2) 이것들은 신상품 신발들이다. 그것들은 비싸다.

→ _____ are brand-new shoes. _____ are expensive.

3) 저것은 그의 셔츠이다.

→ _____ is his shirt.

06 보기와 같이 주어진 단수 문장을 복수 문장으로 바꾸어 쓰시오.

> **보기**   This is my book. (단수)
> → These are my books. (복수)

1) That is her pencil.

→ _____

2) Is this your suitcase?

→ _____

3) Is that an MP3 player?

→ _____

4) That backpack is very useful.

→ _____

07 주어진 말을 이용하여 다음 우리말을 영작하시오.

1) 겨울이다. (winter)

→ _____

2) 밖이 매우 어둡다. (dark, outside)

→ _____

3) 그 마을 자체가 아름답다. (village, beautiful)

→ _____

4) 이 노트북 컴퓨터는 내 것이다. (laptop computer)

→ _____

5) 케이트(Kate)와 해리(Harry)는 그들 자신을 자랑스러워한다. (be proud of)

→ _____

01 빈칸에 some이나 any 중 알맞은 것을 쓰시오.

1) Would you like to have _____ milk?

2) He wants _____ apple juice.

3) I don't have _____ ideas.

4) Have _____ more cake.

5) Do they have _____ money?

6) There are _____ books in the bookcase.

7) She doesn't eat _____ meat.

8) Don't touch _____ of the paintings.

02 빈칸에 보기의 대명사 중 알맞은 것을 쓰시오.

보기	one	ones	it	them

1) This shirt is too small. Show me another _____.

2) Harry knows the rumor. _____ is shocking.

3) Sally doesn't have a bike. She needs _____.

4) Kevin needs a cup but he doesn't have _____.

5) Paul and Suzie went to a concert and they liked _____.

6) Kate has a pair of shoes. I want the same _____.

7) Kevin has three dogs: one white one and two brown _____.

8) I have a lot of coins. I keep _____ in a piggy bank.

03 다음 문장의 <u>틀린</u> 부분에 밑줄을 긋고 바르게 고쳐 쓰시오.

1) We don't have some chairs.　　　　(→ _____)

2) Her pants are old. She needs new one.　　(→ _____)

3) Would you like any ice cream?　　　(→ _____)

4) He has a toy car and he likes one.　　(→ _____)

5) Do you have some pens?　　　　(→ _____)

6) There is any water in the bottle.　　(→ _____)

7) We need a fan. Do you have it?　　(→ _____)

8) He has any sneakers.　　　　　(→ _____)

04 우리말과 일치하도록 빈칸에 알맞은 대명사를 쓰시오.

1) 수잔의 차는 고장났다. 그녀는 새 것이 필요하다.

→ Susan's car is broken down. She needs a new _____.

2) 우산 좀 가지고 있나요?

→ Do you have _____ umbrellas?

3) 케이트는 새 원피스를 하나 원한다. 그녀는 빨간 것을 찾고 있다.

→ Kate wants a new dress. She is looking for a red _____.

4) 수지는 한국에 친구가 한 명도 없다.

→ Suzie doesn't have _____ friends in Korea.

5) 나는 검은 장갑이 마음에 들지 않는다. 나는 빨간 것을 원한다.

→ I don't like black gloves. I want red _____.

6) 꽃병에 꽃 몇 송이가 있다.

→ There are _____ flowers in the vase.

7) 나는 만화책을 한 권 읽고 있다. 그것은 재미있다.

→ I'm reading a comic book. _____ is funny.

8) 샐리는 양말 한 켤레를 가지고 있다. 그것들은 새것이다.

→ Sally has a pair of socks. _____ are new.

05 주어진 말을 이용하여 다음 우리말을 영작하시오.

1) 케빈(Kevin)은 사진을 한 장도 찍지 않는다. (take pictures)

→ _____

2) 쿠키 좀 드시겠어요? (would you like, cookies)

→ _____

3) 당신은 나쁜 버릇을 좀 가지고 있나요? (bad habits)

→ _____

4) 그는 소설책이 몇 권 있다. (novels)

→ _____

5) 나는 연필이 하나도 없어. 너는 연필을 가지고 있니? (one)

→ _____

6) 나의 반 친구들 중 몇 명은 인도 출신이다. (India)

→ _____

O1 다음 형용사를 부사형으로 바꾸시오.

1) angry   → _____

2) slow   → _____

3) nice   → _____

4) easy   → _____

5) beautiful → _____

6) early   → _____

7) hard   → _____

8) safe   → _____

9) strange → _____

10) soft   → _____

O2 다음 문장의 <u>틀린</u> 부분에 밑줄을 긋고 바르게 고쳐 쓰시오.

1) Kate speaks English fastly.   (→ _____)

2) Harry always is kind to people.   (→ _____)

3) They feel often tired.   (→ _____)

4) We made Mom happily.   (→ _____)

5) He doesn't have special anything.   (→ _____)

6) Suzie is a very carefully girl.   (→ _____)

7) You can use sometimes my bike.   (→ _____)

8) He is a student clever.   (→ _____)

9) Sally looks nicely.   (→ _____)

10) Amy is sadly.   (→ _____)

O3 우리말과 일치하도록 주어진 말과 보기의 빈도부사를 이용하여 문장을 완성하시오.

| 보기 | always | usually | often | sometimes | never |

1) 수지는 항상 바쁘다. (busy)

→ Suzie _____ busy.

2) 해리는 그의 친구들과 절대 싸우지 않는다. (fight with)

→ Harry _____ his friends.

3) 폴은 자주 고기를 요리한다. (cook)

→ Paul _____ meat.

4) 존은 주말에 대개 집에 있는다. (be at home)

→ John _____ on weekends.

5) 줄리는 때때로 샘에게 전화한다. (call)

→ Julie _____ Sam.

04 주어진 단어를 알맞은 위치에 넣어 문장을 다시 쓰시오.

1) Harry is generous. (always)

→ _____

2) Kate will see John again. (never)

→ _____

3) Suzie's grandmother goes to church on Sunday. (usually)

→ _____

4) Emma is late for school. (often)

→ _____

5) Susan can take a trip. (sometimes)

→ _____

6) James drinks coffee. (never)

→ _____

05 밑줄 친 부분에 유의하여 다음 문장을 해석하시오.

1) Suzie swims fast.

→ _____

2) Suzie is a fast swimmer.

→ _____

3) Harry wakes up early.

→ _____

4) Harry had an early breakfast.

→ _____

06 주어진 말을 이용하여 다음 우리말을 영작하시오.

1) 글로리아(Gloria)는 무언가 맛있는 것을 가지고 있다. (delicious, something)

→ _____

2) 나의 언니는 절대 울지 않는다. (cry)

→ _____

3) 엄마는 매우 천천히 차를 운전한다. (drive her car)

→ _____

4) 그는 항상 늦게 일어난다. (get up)

→ _____

01 다음 형용사의 비교급과 최상급을 쓰시오.

1) cute   – _____ – _____
2) heavy   – _____ – _____
3) hot   – _____ – _____
4) famous – _____ – _____
5) dirty   – _____ – _____
6) kind   – _____ – _____

02 다음 중 알맞은 것을 고르시오.

1) Susan is   very | much   stronger than Emma.
2) Harry is as   heavy | heavier   as Tom.
3) Emma is   more healthier | healthier   than Jane.
4) Jerry is the cleverest   in | of   all.
5) Suzie is the   smarter | smartest   girl in my class.
6) A car is   more comfortable | comfortabler   than a bus.
7) This room is   more noisy | noisier   than that one.
8) Cindy is one of   the prettiest girl | the prettiest girls   in my club.

03 우리말과 일치하도록 주어진 단어를 알맞게 고쳐 쓰시오.

1) 이 책은 저 책만큼 두껍지 않다. (thick)
   → This book is not as _____ as that one.

2) 레이첼은 우리 반에서 제일 부지런한 학생이다. (diligent)
   → Rachel is _____ student in our class.

3) 이 기계는 저 기계보다 더 유용하다. (useful)
   → This machine is _____ than that one.

4) 이 탁자는 저 탁자보다 더 크다. (big)
   → This table is _____ than that one.

5) 케이트는 제인만큼 아름답다. (beautiful)
   → Kate is as _____ as Jane.

6) 수잔의 목소리는 제리의 목소리보다 훨씬 더 부드럽다. (soft)
   → Susan's voice is _____ than Jerry's.

O4 다음 문장을 우리말로 해석하시오.

1) This car is not as fast as that one.

→ _____

2) Suzie is much wiser than Jane.

→ _____

3) This is the oldest building in this city.

→ _____

4) Mt. Everest is higher than Mt. Kilimanjaro.

→ _____

O5 우리말과 일치하도록 주어진 단어를 알맞게 배열하시오.

1) 이 책은 그 책보다 훨씬 더 비싸다. (than, this, much, one, expensive, that, is, more, book)

→ _____

2) 제인은 로라만큼 용감하지 않다. (Jane, as, is, Laura, brave, as, not)

→ _____

3) 그는 세계에서 가장 뛰어난 야구 선수들 중 한 명이다.
(the, players, one, is, the, world, baseball, he, of, best, in)

→ _____

4) 케빈은 팀보다 말랐다. (Tim, is, than, Kevin, thinner)

→ _____

O6 주어진 말을 이용하여 다음 우리말을 영작하시오.

1) 그는 우리나라에서 가장 웃긴 코미디언이다. (funny, comedian)

→ _____

2) 영어는 한국어만큼 중요하다. (important)

→ _____

3) 이 교실은 저 교실보다 더 크다. (big)

→ _____

4) 제임스(James)는 우리 학교에서 가장 바쁜 학생들 중 한 명이다. (busy)

→ _____

5) 케이트(Kate)는 제인(Jane)보다 훨씬 더 호기심이 많다. (curious)

→ _____

01 문장의 주어와 동사에 밑줄 긋고 보기처럼 표시하시오.

> 보기 The <u>sun</u> <u>shines</u> brightly.
>   주어   동사

1) Mr. Baker cooks well.

2) Mr. Lee teaches us English.

3) Joey and Charles are close friends.

4) My sister Jiwon has long hair.

5) Her hands feel warm.

6) They are playing soccer now.

02 밑줄 친 부분에 해당하는 문장 요소를 쓰시오.

> 보기   주격 보어   목적어   직접목적어   간접목적어   목적격 보어

1) My brother became <u>a movie star</u>.   (_____)
2) Mary looks <u>so cute</u>.   (_____)
3) They play <u>basketball</u> with their friends.   (_____)
4) Mr. and Mrs. Pitt named their daughter <u>Vivien</u>.   (_____)
5) My mother will buy me <u>a new cell phone</u>.   (_____)
6) She lent <u>Mary</u> her notebook.   (_____)

03 밑줄 친 문장 요소들을 보기처럼 표시하시오.

> 보기 <u>My mother</u> <u>teaches</u> <u>French</u>.
>   주어   동사   목적어

1) <u>The woman</u> <u>works</u> hard.

2) <u>They</u> <u>aren't</u> <u>expensive</u>.

3) <u>Mr. and Mrs. Johnson</u> <u>have</u> <u>two sons</u>.

4) <u>He</u> <u>made</u> <u>his daughter</u> <u>a white dress</u>.

5) <u>She</u> <u>calls</u> <u>her puppy</u> <u>Spike</u>.

04 우리말과 일치하도록 주어진 단어를 알맞게 배열하시오.

1) 그는 일주일에 두 번 스페인어 수업을 듣는다. (twice, a, lessons, week, Spanish, takes, he)

→ _____

2) 우리는 그 고양이를 '키티'라고 부른다. (cat, call, we, the, Kitty)

→ _____

3) 그녀는 무서운 영화를 좋아하지 않는다. (does, like, movies, scary, she, not)

→ _____

4) 내 양말은 서랍 속에 없다. (socks, in, my, are, drawer, the, not)

→ _____

5) 나는 나의 어머니께 이 꽃을 사드릴 것이다. (will, buy, my, I, flower, mother, this)

→ _____

6) 나의 언니는 매일 커피를 한 잔 마신다. (sister, cup, my, drinks, a, coffee, day, of, every)

→ _____

7) 내 남동생의 실수는 나를 화나게 했다. (mistake, my, made, angry, me, brother's)

→ _____

8) 그들은 영국에서 가장 유명한 밴드가 되었다. (became, in, band, England, most, they, the, famous)

→ _____

05 주어진 말을 이용하여 다음 우리말을 영작하시오.

1) 그녀는 그녀의 친구와 이야기하고 있다. (talk to)

→ _____

2) 우리는 수요일에 4교시 수업이 있다. (Wednesday)

→ _____

3) 그의 노래는 우리를 슬프게 한다. (sad)

→ _____

4) 나는 그의 생일에 그에게 선물을 준다. (present)

→ _____

5) 그 천은 부드럽게 느껴진다. (cloth)

→ _____

6) 나는 그에게 편지 한 통을 썼다. (wrote)

→ _____

01 다음 중 알맞은 것을 고르시오.

1) There [is | are] a bag on the bench.

2) There [is | are] a lot of coffee in the café.

3) Are there a lot of [milk | apples] on the table?

4) There [isn't | aren't] any bread in the bakery.

5) [Is | Are] there any students in the classroom?

6) There [is | are] a lot of books on the bookshelf.

7) There is [a bear | some bears] in the zoo.

02 우리말과 일치하도록 빈칸에 알맞은 말을 쓰시오.

1) 정원에는 많은 꽃들이 있다.

→ _____ _____ many _____ in the garden.

2) 책상 위에 약간의 종이가 있다.

→ _____ _____ some paper on the desk.

3) 병 안에 설탕이 많지 않다.

→ _____ _____ much sugar in the bottle.

4) 거리에는 많은 자동차가 있습니까?

→ _____ _____ many _____ on the street?

5) 이 마을에는 공원이 있습니까?

→ _____ _____ a _____ in this village?

6) 이 동물원에는 사람들이 많지 않다.

→ There _____ _____ many people in this zoo.

03 다음 질문에 대한 대답을 완성하시오.

1) Ⓐ Are there many children there?　　Ⓑ Yes, _____ _____.

2) Ⓐ Are there any oranges on the table?　　Ⓑ No, _____ _____.

3) Ⓐ Is there a bed in your room?　　Ⓑ No, _____ _____.

4) Ⓐ Is there a pear in the basket?　　Ⓑ Yes, _____ _____.

04 다음 문장을 지시대로 바꾸어 쓰시오.

1) There are some pictures on the wall.
부정문 ▶ _____

2) There is a lot of salt in the kitchen.
부정문 ▶ _____

3) There are a lot of windows in this house.
의문문 ▶ _____

4) There is a cap in the drawer.
의문문 ▶ _____

05 다음 문장의 틀린 부분에 밑줄을 긋고 바르게 고쳐 쓰시오.

1) There is four people in my family. (→ _____)

2) Is there many fast food restaurants around us? (→ _____)

3) There isn't any stars in the sky. (→ _____)

4) Ⓐ Is there any butter in the refrigerator? Ⓑ Yes, it is. (→ _____)

5) Ⓐ Are there any trees in your house? Ⓑ No, they aren't. (→ _____)

06 주어진 말을 이용하여 다음 우리말을 영작하시오.

1) 거리를 따라 많은 꽃들이 있다. (a lot of, along the street)
→ _____

2) 사막에는 충분한 물이 없다. (enough, desert)
→ _____

3) 나의 지갑에는 돈이 하나도 없다. (purse)
→ _____

4) 한국에는 많은 산들이 있습니까? (many)
→ _____

5) 이 주변에 병원이 있습니까? (hospital, around here)
→ _____

6) 이 호수 안에는 많은 물고기들이 있다. (a lot of, lake)
→ _____

01 다음 중 알맞은 것을 고르시오.

1) Let's play | plays soccer during break time.

2) Don't | Doesn't throw away the paper.

3) How | What fast time goes by!

4) How | What a big house you have!

5) Let's don't | not watch TV.

6) Is | Be kind to others.

02 우리말과 일치하도록 빈칸에 알맞은 말을 쓰시오.

1) 보라야, 너의 책을 펴라.

→ Bora, _____ your book.

2) 그 안에 너무 많은 기름을 넣지 말아라.

→ _____ _____ too much oil in it.

3) 착한 학생이 되어라.

→ _____ a good student.

4) 슬퍼하지 말아라.

→ _____ _____ sad.

5) 이 컴퓨터를 사용하자.

→ _____ _____ this computer.

6) 야구를 하지 말자.

→ _____ _____ _____ baseball.

03 다음 문장을 지시대로 바꾸어 쓰시오.

1) You are an honest man.

　명령문 ▶ _____

2) Open the window.

　부정 명령문 ▶ _____

3) You love plants and animals.

　명령문 ▶ _____

4) Let's go to the library.

　부정문 ▶ _____

04 주어진 단어를 사용하여 다음 문장을 감탄문으로 바꾸어 쓰시오.

1) The bell is very old. (how)

→ _____

2) This is a very expensive bag. (what)

→ _____

3) They are very handsome boys. (what)

→ _____

4) Your sister dances very well. (how)

→ _____

5) Your socks are very colorful. (how)

→ _____

05 다음 문장의 <u>틀린</u> 부분에 밑줄을 긋고 바르게 고쳐 쓰시오.

1) Tom, reads these books.　　　　　(→ _____)

2) Aren't be late for school.　　　　(→ _____)

3) Let's don't waste paper.　　　　 (→ _____)

4) What nice the weather is!　　　　(→ _____)

5) How beautiful flowers they are!　 (→ _____)

6) Not touch these pictures.　　　　(→ _____)

06 주어진 말을 이용하여 다음 우리말을 영작하시오.

1) 너는 참 멋진 차를 가지고 있구나! (what, nice)

→ _____

2) 내 휴대전화를 사용하지 말아라. (cell phone)

→ _____

3) 전등을 켜 주세요. (turn on)

→ _____

4) 그 개를 두려워하지 말아라. (afraid of)

→ _____

5) 그 피자 정말 맛있구나! (how, delicious)

→ _____

6) 이 스웨터를 사자. (sweater)

→ _____

01 다음 중 알맞은 것을 고르시오.

1) You learned to ski, don't you | didn't you ?

2) Jenny runs so fast, doesn't she | isn't she ?

3) Your sister can play tennis, can she | can't she ?

4) This is not a cheap bag, is this | is it ?

5) The dogs are so cute, aren't the dog | aren't they ?

02 우리말과 일치하도록 빈칸에 알맞은 말을 쓰시오.

1) 너는 그것을 이해하지 못해, 그렇지?

→ You _____ understand it, do _____ ?

2) 이 서점은 일요일에는 문을 닫아, 그렇지 않아?

→ This bookstore closes on Sunday, _____ _____ ?

3) 너의 여동생은 수영을 할 수 있어, 그렇지 않아?

→ Your sister _____ swim, can't _____ ?

4) 같이 노래 부르자, 그럴래?

→ Let's sing together, _____ _____ ?

5) 그 남자는 커피를 마시고 있어, 그렇지 않아?

→ The man is drinking coffee, _____ _____ ?

03 다음 문장 뒤에 알맞은 부가의문문을 쓰시오.

1) You go to bed at 10, _____ _____ ?

2) My parents watched the movie last Saturday, _____ _____ ?

3) Your father can play golf, _____ _____ ?

4) He is not playing the drum, _____ _____ ?

5) The kids didn't read books last night, _____ _____ ?

6) The movies are not boring, _____ _____ ?

7) There are some pictures on the wall, _____ _____ ?

8) Clean your room, _____ _____ ?

9) Let's go on a picnic, _____ _____ ?

10) Mr. Smith will come back soon, _____ _____ ?

04 다음 질문에 대한 대답을 완성하시오.

1) Ⓐ You can skate, can't you? Ⓑ Yes, _____ _____.

2) Ⓐ Mr. Kim arrived here, didn't he? Ⓑ No, _____ _____.

3) Ⓐ The bag is useful, isn't it? Ⓑ Yes, _____ _____.

4) Ⓐ Let's take a walk, shall we? Ⓑ Yes, _____.

05 다음 우리말을 영어로 표현할 때 틀린 부분에 밑줄을 긋고 바르게 고쳐 쓰시오.

1) 그들은 여행을 많이 다녀, 그렇지 않아?

They travel a lot, doesn't they? (→ _____)

2) 너의 여동생은 자전거를 탈 수 있어, 그렇지 않아?

Your sister can ride a bike, can't you? (→ _____)

3) 그녀는 그를 사랑하지 않아, 그렇지?

She does not love him, doesn't she? (→ _____)

4) 그 병원 근처에는 공원이 있어, 그렇지 않아?

There is a park near the hospital, isn't it? (→ _____)

5) 너의 아버지는 지금 일하고 계셔, 그렇지 않아?

Your father is working now, doesn't he? (→ _____)

6) 너는 유학을 가지 않을 거야, 그렇지?

You won't go abroad, do you? (→ _____)

06 주어진 말을 이용하여 다음 우리말을 영작하시오.

1) 날씨가 무척 더워, 그렇지 않아? (hot)

→ _____

2) 네 친구들은 어젯밤에 운전을 하지 않았어, 그렇지? (drive)

→ _____

3) 너의 할머니는 꽃을 좋아하셔, 그렇지 않아? (flowers)

→ _____

4) 너의 남동생은 지금 숙제를 하고 있지 않아, 그렇지? (do one's homework)

→ _____

5) 너의 어머니는 교회에 다니셔, 그렇지 않아? (church)

→ _____

6) 서울은 큰 도시야, 그렇지 않아? (city)

→ _____

01 다음 중 알맞은 것을 고르시오.

1) Mr. Baker is | are | was | were in America last month.

2) They wasn't | weren't | aren't | isn't busy last week.

3) Once there is | are | was | were a handsome prince.

4) The books is | am | was | were very exciting.

5) Was | Were | Are | Is you at home yesterday?

6) The students is | are | was | were in the classroom an hour ago.

02 우리말과 일치하도록 빈칸에 알맞은 말을 쓰시오.

1) 어제는 매우 추웠다.

→ It _____ very cold yesterday.

2) 우리는 한 시간 전에 배가 고프지 않았다.

→ We _____ hungry an hour _____.

3) 나는 어제 학교에 지각하지 않았다.

→ I _____ _____ late for school yesterday.

4) 그 고양이는 어젯밤에 거리에 있었니?

→ _____ the cat on the street _____ night?

5) 그녀의 아들들은 지난해에 영국에 있었니?

→ _____ her sons in England _____ _____?

03 다음 문장을 지시대로 바꾸어 쓰시오.

1) His parents were in Jejudo last weekend.

부정문 ▶ _____

2) My father was happy with my grades.

부정문 ▶ _____

3) It was rainy in Seoul yesterday.

의문문 ▶ _____

4) They were at the mall this morning.

의문문 ▶ _____

04 다음 질문에 대한 대답을 완성하시오.

1) **A** Was your mother in the room?　　　　**B** Yes, _____ _____.

2) **A** Were your parents happy with it?　　　**B** No, _____ _____.

3) **A** Was your brother angry?　　　　　　**B** Yes, _____ _____.

4) **A** Were you in the library yesterday?　　**B** No, _____ _____.

5) **A** Was yesterday Sunday?　　　　　　　**B** No, _____ _____.

6) **A** Were there two puppies there?　　　　**B** Yes, _____ _____.

05 다음 우리말을 영어로 표현할 때 <u>틀린</u> 부분에 밑줄을 긋고 바르게 고쳐 쓰시오.

1) 그들은 지난 주에 대전에 있었니?

Are they in Daejeon last week?　　　　　　　　　(→ _____)

2) 브라운 부부는 어제 집에 있었다.

Mr. and Mrs. Brown was at home yesterday.　　　(→ _____)

3) 그녀의 머리카락은 작년에는 길었었다.

Her hair are long last year.　　　　　　　　　　(→ _____)

4) 어젯밤에는 길에 자동차가 많지 않았다.

There are not many cars on the road last night.　　(→ _____)

5) **A** 너의 언니는 작년에 15살이었니?　　**B** 응, 그래.

A Was your sister 15 years old last year?　**B** Yes, she is.　(→ _____)

6) 5년 전에는 마을에 공장들이 많이 있었다.

There is a lot of factories in the town five years ago.　(→ _____)

06 주어진 말을 이용하여 다음 우리말을 영작하시오.

1) 어제는 나의 생일이었다. (birthday)

→ _____

2) 캐시(Cathy)와 밥(Bob)은 작년에 초등학생이 아니었다. (elementary school student)

→ _____

3) 나의 아버지는 10년 전에는 날씬했다. (thin)

→ _____

4) 너의 어머니는 어제 출근하셨니? (at work)

→ _____

5) 그 아이들은 한 시간 전에 교실에 없었다. (classroom)

→ _____

O1 다음 동사의 과거형을 바르게 쓰시오.

1) live   – _____

2) stop   – _____

3) try   – _____

4) plan   – _____

5) enjoy – _____

6) teach – _____

7) see   – _____

8) take   – _____

O2 우리말과 일치하도록 빈칸에 알맞은 말을 쓰시오.

1) 보미는 오늘 아침 일찍 일어났다.

   → Bomi _____ up early this morning.

2) 나의 언니는 작년에 수영을 배웠다.

   → My sister _____ to swim last year.

3) 나는 어젯밤 저녁을 먹은 후에 설거지를 하지 않았다.

   → I _____ _____ the dishes after dinner last night.

4) 그들은 어제 저녁을 먹지 않았다.

   → They _____ _____ _____ dinner yesterday.

5) 너의 아버지는 일하러 가셨니?

   → _____ your father _____ to work?

O3 다음 문장을 지시대로 바꾸어 쓰시오.

1) They picked up the trash.

   부정문▶ _____

2) My brother did his homework.

   부정문▶ _____

3) He took his sister to the museum.

   의문문▶ _____

4) They played soccer after school.

   의문문▶ _____

5) It snowed last night.

   의문문▶ _____

04 다음 질문에 대한 대답을 완성하시오.

1) **A** Did you finish the work? **B** Yes, _____ _____.

2) **A** Did Mr. Kim speak to you? **B** No, _____ _____.

3) **A** Did your brothers read the book? **B** Yes, _____ _____.

05 주어진 말을 이용하여 다음 질문에 대한 대답을 쓰시오.

1) **A** What did you do after school?

B _____ (play table tennis)

2) **A** What did your mother do yesterday?

B _____ (have a party)

06 다음 우리말을 영어로 표현할 때 틀린 부분에 밑줄을 긋고 바르게 고쳐 쓰시오.

1) 나의 어머니와 나는 작년에 스페인을 방문했다.

My mother and I visit Spain last year. (→ _____)

2) 캐런은 그저께 버스에 그녀의 지갑을 두고 왔다.

Karen leaved her purse on the bus the day before yesterday. (→ _____)

3) 보라는 어제 방을 청소하지 않았다.

Bora does not cleaned her room yesterday. (→ _____)

4) 그는 지난 일요일에 체육관에 갔니?

Was he go to the gym last Sunday? (→ _____)

5) 유나는 며칠 전에 나에게 피자를 만들어 주었다.

Yuna makes pizza for me a few days ago. (→ _____)

07 주어진 말을 이용하여 다음 우리말을 영작하시오.

1) 나의 아버지는 어젯밤에 낚시하러 갔다. (go fishing)

→ _____

2) 나는 어제 야구를 하지 않았다. (baseball)

→ _____

3) 크리스(Chris)는 며칠 전에 나비 한 마리를 잡았니? (catch, butterfly, a few days ago)

→ _____

4) 로렌(Lauren)은 작년에 수학을 열심히 공부했다. (math)

→ _____

5) 그녀는 그녀의 부모님과 함께 일본을 방문하지 않았다. (visit)

→ _____

01 다음 중 알맞은 것을 고르시오.

1) I have never   meet | met   a famous person.

2) She and he   have | has   eaten Mexican food before.

3) She   helped | has helped   poor people since then.

4) Have you ever   do | done | did   any volunteer work?

5) We   have played | played   soccer last weekend.

6) He   hasn't | didn't   cleaned the house yet.

7) My father   has gone | went   to Germany two days ago.

8) My parents   were | have been   busy since last Monday.

02 현재완료시제에 유의하여 다음 문장을 우리말로 해석하시오.

1) He has played the flute for two hours.

→ _____

2) She has not washed the dishes yet.

→ _____

3) Mary has been at the library since 5 o'clock.

→ _____

4) It has been snowy since yesterday.

→ _____

5) The train for Busan has just left.

→ _____

6) Has he ever seen a real kangaroo before?

→ _____

03 두 문장이 같은 뜻이 되도록 빈칸을 알맞게 채우시오.

1) She lost her cat and she still doesn't have it.

= She _____ _____ her cat.

2) They went to Jejudo and they are not back yet.

= They _____ _____ to Jejudo.

3) My sister was sick yesterday and she is still sick now.

= My sister _____ _____ sick since yesterday.

정답 및 해설 p.29

04 다음 질문에 대한 대답을 완성하시오.

1) Ⓐ Have you ever been to Paris?　　Ⓑ Yes, _____ _____.

2) Ⓐ Has Jenny finished the work?　　Ⓑ No, _____ _____.

05 주어진 말을 이용하여 다음 질문에 대한 대답을 쓰시오.

1) Ⓐ What have you done?

Ⓑ _____ (wash the car)

2) Ⓐ What has your sister done since 2 o'clock?

Ⓑ _____ (study English)

06 다음 우리말을 영어로 표현할 때 **틀린** 부분에 밑줄을 긋고 바르게 고쳐 쓰시오.

1) 그녀는 작년에 그 차를 사고 싶었다.

She has wanted to buy that car last year.　　　(→ _____)

2) 브라운 부부는 어제부터 계속 집에 있었다.

Mr. and Mrs. Brown were at home since yesterday.　　(→ _____)

3) 그들은 그 소문을 들어본 적이 없다.

They never have heard that rumor.　　　(→ _____)

4) 우리는 이미 목욕을 했다.

We have already take a bath.　　　(→ _____)

5) 캐런은 전에 한 번 캐나다에 가본 적이 있다.

Karen has be to Canada once before.　　　(→ _____)

6) 그녀와 나는 일주일 전에 그 영화를 보았다.

She and I have watched the movie a week ago.　　(→ _____)

07 주어진 말을 이용하여 다음 우리말을 영작하시오.

1) 나는 아프리카에 가본 적이 없다. (Africa)

→ _____

2) 그녀는 그 개를 지난해부터 키우고 있다. (keep a dog)

→ _____

3) 너는 영화배우를 만나본 적이 있니? (movie star)

→ _____

4) 우리는 3일 동안 이 호텔에 머무르고 있다. (stay)

→ _____

01 다음 중 알맞은 것을 고르시오.

1) Ⓐ Who | Whom invited you? — Ⓑ Jiho did.
2) Ⓐ Who | Which is cheaper, this pen or that one? — Ⓑ This pen is cheaper.
3) Ⓐ Who | Whose car is this? — Ⓑ It's mine.
4) Ⓐ Who | Whose are you talking with? — Ⓑ I am talking with my mom.
5) Ⓐ What | Who does she need? — Ⓑ She needs a cell phone.
6) Ⓐ What | Whose are those? — Ⓑ They are soccer balls.
7) Ⓐ What | Who are they? — Ⓑ They are my parents.
8) Ⓐ What | Whose umbrella is that? — Ⓑ It's Milke's.

02 빈칸에 알맞은 의문사를 쓰시오.

1) Ⓐ _____ is his job? — Ⓑ He is a dentist.
2) Ⓐ _____ house is this? — Ⓑ It's my uncle's house.
3) Ⓐ _____ does she do after school on Mondays? — Ⓑ She takes a piano lesson.
4) Ⓐ _____ is that girl over there? — Ⓑ She is my sister.
5) Ⓐ _____ is heavier, the box or the bag? — Ⓑ The box is heavier.
6) Ⓐ _____ _____ is it? — Ⓑ It is Friday.
7) Ⓐ _____ _____ is your car? — Ⓑ It is gray.
8) Ⓐ _____ _____ does your brother get up? — Ⓑ He gets up at 7 o'clock.

03 다음 문장이 같은 뜻이 되도록 빈칸을 채우시오.

1) What time is it now?
= What's _____ _____?
= _____ time do you _____?
= Do you have _____ _____?

2) What does your father do for a living?
= What is your father's _____?

3) Whose toy is this?
= _____ is this toy?

4) Whom do you like?
= _____ do you like?

04 다음 문장의 밑줄 친 부분을 바르게 고쳐 쓰시오.

1) Ⓐ Whose is this watch?　　Ⓑ It is my brother.　　(→ _____)

2) Ⓐ What's the date?　　Ⓑ It is Saturday.　　(→ _____)

3) Ⓐ Do you have the time?　　Ⓑ Yes, I do. It is nine.　　(→ _____)

4) Ⓐ Who is taller, Suji and Mina?　　Ⓑ Suji is.　　(→ _____)

05 주어진 말을 이용하여 다음 질문에 대한 대답을 쓰시오.

1) Ⓐ What does your brother do at night?

　　Ⓑ _____ (play computer games)

2) Ⓐ Whose bicycle is this?

　　Ⓑ _____ (my sister)

3) Ⓐ What day is it today?

　　Ⓑ _____ (Wednesday)

4) Ⓐ What time is it now?

　　Ⓑ _____ (three thirty)

06 다음 문장의 밑줄 친 부분이 대답이 되도록 의문문을 쓰시오.

1) He met Bora yesterday.

　→ _____

2) My grandmother is talking on the phone.

　→ _____

3) She has some peanuts in her hand.

　→ _____

07 주어진 말을 이용하여 다음 우리말을 영작하시오.

1) 누가 이 나무를 심었나요? (plant)

　→ _____

2) 이 고양이는 누구의 것입니까?

　→ _____

3) 너의 할아버지는 일요일에 뭐하시니?

　→ _____

4) 이 컴퓨터와 저 컴퓨터 중에서 어느 것이 더 좋니? (computer)

　→ _____

01 다음 중 알맞은 것을 고르시오.

1) Ⓐ How | When are you today?   Ⓑ I am good.

2) Ⓐ When | Where is your mother?   Ⓑ She is in her car.

3) Ⓐ How | Why do you go to school?   Ⓑ I go to school by bike.

4) Ⓐ Why | When was he born?   Ⓑ He was born in 1988.

5) Ⓐ How | Why is the baby crying?   Ⓑ Because she is hungry.

6) Ⓐ When | Where do you work?   Ⓑ I work at a bank.

02 빈칸에 알맞은 의문사를 쓰시오.

1) Ⓐ _____ is his birthday?   Ⓑ It's on March 2.

2) Ⓐ _____ does your uncle live?   Ⓑ He lives in Pohang.

3) Ⓐ _____ is the weather outside? Ⓑ It is snowing.

4) Ⓐ _____ does the bus leave?   Ⓑ It leaves at seven thirty.

5) Ⓐ _____ do you like him?   Ⓑ Because he is smart and kind.

6) Ⓐ _____ did he go to Jejudo?   Ⓑ He went there by plane.

7) Ⓐ _____ are my glasses?   Ⓑ They are on your desk.

8) Ⓐ _____ was your trip?   Ⓑ It was really great.

03 주어진 말을 이용하여 다음 질문에 대한 대답을 쓰시오.

1) Ⓐ Why does he feel happy?

   Ⓑ _____ (today, birthday)

2) Ⓐ Where are you going to study?

   Ⓑ _____ (the library)

3) Ⓐ When did you go to France?

   Ⓑ _____ (two years ago)

4) Ⓐ How does your sister go to church?

   Ⓑ _____ (subway)

5) Ⓐ Where is my school uniform?

   Ⓑ _____ (in the washing machine)

04 다음 문장의 밑줄 친 부분이 대답이 되도록 의문문을 쓰시오.

1) He met his wife <u>five years ago</u>.

    → _____

2) They play soccer <u>on the playground</u>.

    → _____

3) She went to the museum <u>by bus</u>.

    → _____

4) I like the dress <u>because it is very pretty</u>.

    → _____

05 밑줄 친 문장을 바르게 고쳐 쓰시오.

1) Ⓐ <u>Where does the class start?</u>   Ⓑ It starts at 9 o'clock.

    (→ _____)

2) Ⓐ <u>Why did you come here?</u>   Ⓑ On foot.

    (→ _____)

3) Ⓐ <u>How is the weather like?</u>   Ⓑ It is cloudy and windy.

    (→ _____)

4) Ⓐ Where is the nearest bank?   Ⓑ <u>Yes, It is around the corner.</u>

                                              (→ _____)

5) Ⓐ <u>How do you study so hard?</u>   Ⓑ To get good grades.

    (→ _____)

06 주어진 말을 이용하여 다음 우리말을 영작하시오.

1) 제가 어떻게 불쌍한 아이들을 도울 수 있을까요? (poor)

    → _____

2) 왜 이 책이 중요합니까? (important)

    → _____

3) 당신은 매일 어디에서 테니스를 칩니까? (every day)

    → _____

4) 너의 아버지는 언제 세차를 하셨니? (wash his car)

    → _____

Unit 21 ▶ How + 형용사/부사 ~?

01 다음 중 알맞은 것을 고르시오.

1) Ⓐ How old | How tall is your sister?　　Ⓑ She is ten years old.

2) Ⓐ How much | How tall is your mother?　　Ⓑ She is about 5 feet tall.

3) Ⓐ How many | How much is the bag?　　Ⓑ It is 50,000 won.

4) Ⓐ How far | How high is it from Seoul?　　Ⓑ It is ten kilometers.

5) Ⓐ How many | How much cousins do you have?　　Ⓑ I have two.

6) Ⓐ How long | How often do you come here?　　Ⓑ Twice a week.

7) Ⓐ How many milk | eggs are there?　　Ⓑ There are ten.

02 빈칸에 알맞은 의문사를 쓰시오.

1) Ⓐ ＿＿＿＿＿＿＿＿ computers does your father have?　　Ⓑ He has one.

2) Ⓐ ＿＿＿＿＿＿＿＿ does it take to go to Jejudo?　　Ⓑ It takes an hour by plane.

3) Ⓐ ＿＿＿＿＿＿＿＿ is it from here to the station?　　Ⓑ It is two blocks.

4) Ⓐ ＿＿＿＿＿＿＿＿ do you meet your boyfriend?　　Ⓑ I meet him once a week.

5) Ⓐ ＿＿＿＿＿＿＿＿ are the twins?　　Ⓑ They are 5 years old.

6) Ⓐ ＿＿＿＿＿＿＿＿ are these blue jeans?　　Ⓑ They are 80 dollars.

7) Ⓐ ＿＿＿＿＿＿＿＿ is the ruler?　　Ⓑ It is 15 centimeters long.

03 우리말과 일치하도록 빈칸에 알맞은 말을 쓰시오.

1) Ⓐ 전철역에서 얼마나 멉니까?

→ ＿＿＿＿＿＿＿＿＿＿ ＿＿＿＿＿＿＿＿＿＿ is it from the subway station?

Ⓑ 걸어서 약 5분 거리입니다.

→ ＿＿＿＿＿＿＿＿＿＿ ＿＿＿＿＿＿＿＿＿＿ about a 5-minute walk.

2) Ⓐ 너의 집에는 고양이가 몇 마리 있니?

→ ＿＿＿＿＿＿＿＿＿＿ ＿＿＿＿＿＿＿＿＿＿ ＿＿＿＿＿＿＿＿＿＿ are there in your house?

Ⓑ 두 마리 있어.

→ ＿＿＿＿＿＿＿＿＿＿ ＿＿＿＿＿＿＿＿＿＿ two.

3) Ⓐ 너는 하와이에 얼마 동안 있었니?

→ ＿＿＿＿＿＿＿＿＿＿ ＿＿＿＿＿＿＿＿＿＿ were you in Hawaii?

Ⓑ 나는 그곳에 일주일 동안 있었어.

→ I was there ＿＿＿＿＿＿＿＿＿＿ ＿＿＿＿＿＿＿＿＿＿ ＿＿＿＿＿＿＿＿＿＿.

O4 다음 문장의 밑줄 친 부분이 대답이 되도록 의문문을 쓰시오.

1) He visits his parents <u>once a month</u>.

→ _____

2) My father is <u>45 years old</u>.

→ _____

3) There are <u>three dogs</u>.

→ _____

4) I have <u>ten thousand won</u>.

→ _____

O5 밑줄 친 부분을 바르게 고쳐 쓰시오.

1) Ⓐ <u>How much</u> fish are there in the fishbowl?　　Ⓑ There are three.

(→ _____)

2) Ⓐ <u>How long</u> do you take a shower?　　Ⓑ Every day.

(→ _____)

3) Ⓐ <u>How many</u> butter is there in the refrigerator?　　Ⓑ Not much.

(→ _____)

4) Ⓐ <u>How tall</u> is the baby?　　Ⓑ One year old.

(→ _____)

5) Ⓐ <u>How high</u> is it to the nearest bank?　　Ⓑ Not far. Just two blocks.

(→ _____)

O6 주어진 말을 이용하여 다음 우리말을 영작하시오.

1) 교실에는 학생들이 몇 명 있니? (classroom)

→ _____

2) 너는 얼마나 자주 운동을 하니? (exercise)

→ _____

3) 에베레스트 산은 얼마나 높습니까? (Mt. Everest)

→ _____

4) 거기에 가는 데 얼마나 걸립니까? (take, get there)

→ _____

01 다음 문장의 **틀린** 부분에 밑줄을 긋고 바르게 고쳐 쓰시오.

1) Can Suzie speaks Spanish?   (→ _____)

2) Tom and Jerry were able find it.   (→ _____)

3) The news may be not true.   (→ _____)

4) May I sat here?   (→ _____)

5) Can I going now?   (→ _____)

6) Sally can be able to run fast.   (→ _____)

7) Susan was able not to wait for John.   (→ _____)

8) You borrow can my book.   (→ _____)

02 다음 문장을 우리말로 해석하시오.

1) Kelly can play the piano.

→ _____

2) The story can be true.

→ _____

3) The answer may not be correct.

→ _____

4) You may use my bike.

→ _____

5) She may be a new teacher.

→ _____

6) You can go to the party.

→ _____

03 다음 질문에 대한 대답을 완성하시오.

1) Ⓐ Can I go with you?   Ⓑ Yes, _____ .

2) Ⓐ Can he play the guitar?   Ⓑ No, _____ .

3) Ⓐ Can't she swim?   Ⓑ Yes, _____ .

4) Ⓐ May I ask you a question?   Ⓑ No, _____ _____ .

5) Ⓐ Is she able to ski?   Ⓑ Yes, _____ .

6) Ⓐ Is he able to drive?   Ⓑ No, _____ _____ .

04 다음 문장을 지시대로 바꾸어 쓰시오.

1) Jane can play tennis.

부정문 ▶ _____

2) Harry is able to speak English.

의문문 ▶ _____

3) Susan may stay in the room.

의문문 ▶ _____

4) Paul was able to meet Jane yesterday.

부정문 ▶ _____

5) Sophie can watch TV after dinner.

의문문 ▶ _____

05 두 문장이 같은 뜻이 되도록 빈칸을 알맞게 채우시오.

1) Kate can cook delicious pizza. = Kate _____ cook delicious pizza.

2) Harry can't swim. = Harry _____ swim.

3) Can you run a marathon? = _____ run a marathon?

4) They couldn't help Jerry. = They _____ help Jerry.

06 주어진 말을 이용하여 다음 우리말을 영작하시오.

1) 내가 네 샌드위치를 먹어도 되니? (sandwich)

→ _____

2) 너는 내 공을 사용해도 된다.

→ _____

3) 그는 의사선생님일 리 없다. (doctor)

→ _____

4) 나의 남동생은 자전거를 탈 수 없다. (ride a bike)

→ _____

5) 줄리(Julie)는 5년 전에는 불어를 말할 수 있었다. (French)

→ _____

6) 에이미(Amy)는 그 노래를 좋아하지 않을 지도 모른다.

→ _____

01 다음 중 알맞은 것을 고르시오.

1) He must   pass | passes   the exam this time.

2) You   should | have   to clean the garage.

3) You   must not | doesn't have to   make any noise in the library.

4) Jane   has not to | doesn't have to   buy the book.

5) They will   must | have to   move to another city.

6) Harry   must | has to   be lazy.

02 두 문장이 같은 뜻이 되도록 빈칸에 알맞은 말을 쓰시오.

1) Paul must work on Sunday.   =   Paul _____ work on Sunday.

2) We must remember the password.   =   We _____ remember the password.

3) Suzie doesn't have to cook.   =   Suzie _____ cook.

03 다음 문장을 지시대로 바꾸어 쓰시오.

1) Kate has to leave early in the morning.
   부정문 ▶ _____

2) Paul must give up his plan.
   부정문 ▶ _____

3) They must follow their leader.
   미래형 ▶ _____

4) Harry should go to the library now.
   부정문 ▶ _____

04 우리말과 일치하도록 주어진 단어를 이용하여 문장을 완성하시오.

1) 그녀는 지금 병원에 가야만 하나요?
   → _____ to the hospital now? (must)

2) 너는 야생동물들에게 먹이를 주면 안 된다.
   → You _____ wild animals. (should)

3) 우리는 저녁으로 특별한 무언가를 사야 하나요?
   → _____ something special for dinner? (should)

4) 그 이야기는 사실임에 틀림없다.
   → The story _____ true. (must)

O5 우리말과 일치하도록 주어진 단어를 알맞게 배열하시오.

1) 수지는 선생님임에 틀림없다. (teacher, be, Suzie, a, must)

→ _____

2) 케이트는 규칙적으로 운동해야 한다. (exercise, Kate, should, regularly)

→ _____

3) 제임스는 그 건물에 들어가면 안 된다. (not, building, must, James, the, enter)

→ _____

4) 우리는 어제 일찍 일어나야 했다. (wake, yesterday, had, early, to, we, up)

→ _____

5) 에이미는 그 강아지를 목욕시킬 필요가 없다. (have, dog, wash, Amy, the, to, doesn't)

→ _____

O6 다음 문장을 우리말로 해석하시오.

1) Suzie has to wait here.

→ _____

2) You must not park your car here.

→ _____

3) Kevin will have to buy a train ticket tomorrow.

→ _____

4) James should not eat ice cream too often.

→ _____

O7 주어진 말을 이용하여 다음 우리말을 영작하시오.

1) 수지(Suzie)는 빨리 달릴 필요가 없다. (run)

→ _____

2) 당신은 여기에서 불을 피우면 절대 안됩니다. (make a fire)

→ _____

3) 우리는 그 프로젝트를 지난주에 끝내야 했다. (finish the project)

→ _____

4) 너는 더 천천히 먹어야 한다. (should, more slowly)

→ _____

01 다음 문장의 <u>틀린</u> 부분에 밑줄을 긋고 바르게 고쳐 쓰시오.

1) Harry going to come back soon.   (→ _____)

2) Jane will dance not with John.   (→ _____)

3) Kate is going to coming to the party.   (→ _____)

4) Suzie will plans a trip.   (→ _____)

5) Susan is going learn Spanish.   (→ _____)

6) Amy will be going to visit the museum.   (→ _____)

02 다음 문장을 지시대로 바꾸어 쓰시오.

1) Susan will meet James.

　부정문 ▶ _____

2) Kate and Suzie are going to travel around the world.

　의문문 ▶ _____

3) Amy will have a birthday party.

　의문문 ▶ _____

4) Harry is going to move to New York.

　부정문 ▶ _____

03 주어진 단어를 이용하여 미래시제 문장으로 바꾸어 쓰시오.

1) Kevin is 15 years old. (will, next year)

　→ _____

2) It rains. (be going to, soon)

　→ _____

04 두 문장이 같은 뜻이 되도록 빈칸에 알맞은 말을 쓰시오.

> 보기   Paul will give her a book. = Paul <u>is going to</u> give her a book.

1) Susan will visit her grandparents. = Susan _____ visit her grandparents.

2) James won't make a mistake. = James _____ make a mistake.

3) Amy and Kevin will arrive on time. = Amy and Kevin _____ arrive on time.

4) Will you study in Canada? = _____ study in Canada?

05 다음 질문에 대한 대답을 완성하시오.

1) Ⓐ Will you help us? Ⓑ Yes, _____ _____.
2) Ⓐ Will she write a novel? Ⓑ No, _____ _____.
3) Ⓐ Won't they tell a lie? Ⓑ No, _____ _____.
4) Ⓐ Isn't he going to buy a bike? Ⓑ Yes, _____ _____.
5) Ⓐ Aren't they going to invite him? Ⓑ No, _____ _____.
6) Ⓐ Is she going to visit them? Ⓑ No, _____ _____.

06 다음 문장을 우리말로 해석하시오.

1) Suzie is going to go to Italy.

→ _____

2) Kate is going to Italy now.

→ _____

3) Susan won't touch the painting.

→ _____

4) Amy will join the English book club.

→ _____

07 우리말과 일치하도록 주어진 단어를 알맞게 배열하시오.

1) 해리는 서울로 이사할 예정이다. (is, move, Harry, to, Seoul, to, going)

→ _____

2) 벤은 학교 축제에서 기타를 칠 것이다. (Ben, guitar, play, festival, will, school, the, at, the)

→ _____

3) 케빈은 법을 어기지 않을 것이다. (will, law, Kevin, break, the, not)

→ _____

4) 에이미는 학교 운동회날에 뛸 예정이니? (is, day, on, going, the, sports, school, Amy, run, to)

→ _____

5) 케이트는 그 수업에 등록하지 않을 것이다. (not, to, class, going, Kate, the, is, join)

→ _____

6) 폴이 비밀을 지킬까? (the, keep, Paul, secret, will)

→ _____

01 to부정사에 밑줄을 긋고 명사적 용법에서 무슨 역할인지 보기에서 골라 쓰시오.

보기	주어	목적어	보어

1) Harry wanted to meet his teacher.   (_____)

2) His hobby is to make a music video.   (_____)

3) It is good to make new friends.   (_____)

4) James is planning to go to Paris.   (_____)

5) To play tennis is fun.   (_____)

02 to부정사에 밑줄을 긋고 무슨 용법인지 보기에서 골라 쓰시오.

보기	명사적 용법	형용사적 용법	부사적 용법

1) Kate has a house to live in.   (_____)

2) Suzie will study hard to pass the test.   (_____)

3) I am happy to see Kate.   (_____)

4) Susan has something to drink.   (_____)

5) Jennifer wants to clean her room.   (_____)

03 두 문장이 같은 뜻이 되도록 만드시오.

1) To understand each other is important.

= It _____.

2) To answer the questions will be difficult.

= It _____.

04 다음 문장의 틀린 부분에 밑줄을 긋고 바르게 고쳐 쓰시오.

1) Sally has a book read.   (→ _____)

2) Harry planned learning Chinese.   (→ _____)

3) It is good to speaking English well.   (→ _____)

4) My dream is make a car.   (→ _____)

5) Kate hopes meeting Jane.   (→ _____)

6) Suzie ran catch the bus.   (→ _____)

7) Kevin has something eating.   (→ _____)

8) He will be happy see her.   (→ _____)

05 다음 문장을 우리말로 해석하시오.

1) It is not easy to swim in the sea.

→ _____

2) Harry is planning to travel by train.

→ _____

3) Her hobby is to go to the movies.

→ _____

4) Suzie will go to the library to borrow some books.

→ _____

5) Kate had homework to do.

→ _____

06 우리말과 일치하도록 주어진 단어를 알맞게 배열하시오.

1) 사진을 찍는 것은 멋지다. (pictures, wonderful, take, is, to, it)

→ _____

2) 나는 이야기할 좋은 친구가 있다. (friend, to, I, good, talk, a, have, to)

→ _____

3) 그녀는 놀이공원에 가고 싶어한다. (amusement, go, she, to, an, wants, park, to)

→ _____

4) 그는 그의 친구들을 돕기 위해서 그것을 했다. (friends, to, did, his, he, it, help)

→ _____

07 주어진 말을 이용하여 다음 우리말을 영작하시오.

1) 제시카(Jessica)는 만점을 받기 위해 열심히 공부했다. (a perfect score)

→ _____

2) 그의 꿈은 변호사가 되는 것이다. (lawyer)

→ _____

3) 스티브(Steve)는 새 배낭을 사기를 원한다. (backpack)

→ _____

4) 일찍 자는 것은 좋다. (go to bed, it)

→ _____

5) 나는 읽을 잡지가 하나 있다. (magazine)

→ _____

O1 동명사에 밑줄을 긋고 무슨 역할을 하는지 보기에서 골라 쓰시오.

| 보기 | 주어 | 목적어 | 보어 | 전치사의 목적어 |

1) James gave up smoking.　　　　　　　　(＿＿＿＿＿＿)

2) We talked about running in the race.　　(＿＿＿＿＿＿)

3) My hobby is writing novels.　　　　　　(＿＿＿＿＿＿)

4) Suzie enjoys learning English.　　　　　(＿＿＿＿＿＿)

5) Baking cookies is fun.　　　　　　　　(＿＿＿＿＿＿)

6) Thank you for helping me a lot.　　　　(＿＿＿＿＿＿)

O2 보기에서 알맞은 단어를 골라 빈칸에 to부정사나 동명사 형태로 쓰시오.

| 보기 | invite | fix | learn | dance | become | talk to | play | visit |

1) 해리는 자전거를 고치는 것을 끝냈다.

　→ Harry finished ＿＿＿＿＿＿＿ his bike.

2) 그는 수학자가 되는 것을 계획하고 있다.

　→ He is planning ＿＿＿＿＿＿＿ a mathematician.

3) 초대해 주셔서 감사합니다.

　→ Thank you for ＿＿＿＿＿＿＿ me.

4) 제임스는 농구하는 것을 즐긴다.

　→ James enjoys ＿＿＿＿＿＿＿ basketball.

5) 수잔은 런던을 다시 방문하기를 바란다.

　→ Susan hopes ＿＿＿＿＿＿＿ London again.

6) 줄리아는 춤을 잘 춘다.

　→ Julia is good at ＿＿＿＿＿＿＿.

7) 친구들과 이야기하는 것은 즐겁다.

　→ ＿＿＿＿＿＿＿ friends is fun.

8) 로렌은 프랑스어를 배우기로 결심했다.

　→ Lauren decided ＿＿＿＿＿＿＿ French.

03 다음 문장의 **틀린** 부분에 밑줄을 긋고 바르게 고쳐 쓰시오.

1) Jennifer wants ride a horse.　　　　(→ _____)

2) Harry enjoys cook.　　　　(→ _____)

3) Amy decided join the club.　　　　(→ _____)

4) Suzie finished do her homework.　　　　(→ _____)

5) Kate hopes meet Jane.　　　　(→ _____)

6) Jerry gave up follow them.　　　　(→ _____)

7) Kevin is interested in climb.　　　　(→ _____)

04 우리말과 일치하도록 주어진 단어를 알맞게 배열하시오.

1) 수지는 토요일에 하이킹하는 것을 즐긴다. (hiking, enjoys, Saturday, going, Suzie, on)

→ _____

2) 그녀의 직업은 아이들 옷을 디자인하는 것이다. (clothes, job, designing, her, is, children's)

→ _____

3) TV를 너무 많이 보는 것은 좋지 않다. (TV, not, much, watching, too, good, is)

→ _____

4) 폴은 가구를 만드는 것을 잘한다. (good, Paul, at, making, is, furniture)

→ _____

5) 그들은 다른 도시로 이사하는 것에 대해 이야기했다. (another, moving, they, about, city, talked, to)

→ _____

05 주어진 말을 이용하여 다음 우리말을 영작하시오.

1) 그녀는 여행하는 것을 좋아한다. (be fond of, travel)

→ _____

2) 그의 취미는 피아노를 치는 것이다. (hobby)

→ _____

3) 팸(Pam)은 책을 읽는 것을 끝냈다. (finish)

→ _____

4) 다른 사람들을 돕는 것은 좋다. (others)

→ _____

5) 존(John)은 그림 그리는 것을 즐긴다. (draw pictures)

→ _____

01 다음 중 알맞은 것을 고르시오.

1) Suzie likes fish   and | or | but   doesn't like meat.

2) Kate will see a doctor   so | but | because   she is sick.

3) Which is faster, a car   and | or | but   a train?

4) Jane likes both apples   and | or | but   bananas.

5) Turn left,   and | or | but   you will see the bank.

6) Exercise every day,   and | or | but   you won't be healthy.

7) Amy likes the boy band   because | or | so   she will go to their concert.

02 다음 문장의 틀린 부분에 밑줄을 긋고 바르게 고쳐 쓰시오.

1) 해리는 빨리 뛰었지만 버스를 놓쳤다.

Harry ran fast and missed the bus.   (→ _____)

2) 코트를 입어라, 그렇지 않으면 추울 것이다.

Wear a coat, and you will feel cold.   (→ _____)

3) 열심히 일해라, 그러면 성공할 것이다.

Work hard, or you will succeed.   (→ _____)

4) 날씨가 더워서 우리는 반바지를 입고 있다.

It is hot because we are wearing shorts.   (→ _____)

5) 우리는 돈이 없었기 때문에 집에 걸어갔다.

We walked home so we didn't have any money.   (→ _____)

03 알맞은 접속사를 이용하여 두 문장이 같은 뜻이 되도록 쓰시오.

1) If you hurry up, you will catch the bus.

= Hurry up, _____.

2) If you don't close the window, you may catch a cold.

= Close the window, _____.

3) She is sleepy now because she couldn't sleep last night.

= She couldn't sleep last night, _____.

4) It was hot so we went swimming.

= We went swimming _____.

04 다음 문장을 우리말로 해석하시오.

1) Run fast, and you will win the race.

→ _____

2) Suzie may meet Kate or Paul.

→ _____

3) Eat slowly, or you will have a stomachache.

→ _____

4) Suzie is good at cooking, so she became a cook.

→ _____

5) Kate is smiling because she is happy.

→ _____

05 다음 두 문장을 알맞은 접속사를 사용하여 한 문장으로 만드시오.

1) Kate is wise. She is clever, too.

→ Kate is wise _____.

2) Be kind. People will like you.

→ Be kind, _____.

3) Take a rest. You will be very tired.

→ Take a rest, _____.

4) Susan is sad. She lost her puppy.

→ Susan is sad _____.

06 주어진 말을 이용하여 다음 우리말을 영작하시오.

1) 아침을 먹어라, 그렇지 않으면 너는 배고플 것이다. (hungry)

→ _____

2) 시험은 어려웠다. 그래서 나는 긴장했다. (test, nervous)

→ _____

3) 주디(Judy)는 사과나 딸기나 포도를 먹을 것이다. (apples, strawberries, grapes)

→ _____

4) 션(Sean)은 바빴지만 숙제를 끝마쳤다. (finish)

→ _____

Unit 28 ▶ when, before, after, until

01 다음 중 알맞은 것을 고르시오.

1) Susan is happy   when | until   she meets her friends.

2) Kate sent the email   after | before   she wrote it.

3) Kevin goes to the library   when | after   school.

4) Amy brushes her teeth   after | before   she goes to bed.

5) We will study hard   after | until   we take the exam.

6) Suzie will write a review after she   will read | reads   the book.

02 우리말과 일치하도록 빈칸에 알맞은 말을 쓰시오.

1) 나는 어렸을 때 런던에서 살았다.

→ I lived in London _____ I was a child.

2) 그들은 아침 7시 전에 집에서 나갔다.

→ They left home _____ 7 in the morning.

3) 수잔은 수영을 한 후에 점심을 먹는다.

→ Susan has lunch _____ she swims.

4) 케빈은 잠들기 전에 책을 읽는다.

→ Kevin reads books _____ he goes to bed.

5) 우리는 비가 그칠 때까지 기다렸다.

→ We waited _____ it stopped raining.

03 다음 두 문장을 알맞은 접속사를 이용하여 한 문장으로 만드시오.

1) 눈이 올 때 우리는 눈싸움을 한다. (We have a snowball fight. It snows.)

→ _____

2) 해리는 넘어진 후에 의사를 만났다. (Harry fell down. Harry saw a doctor.)

→ _____

3) 그는 집에 가기 전에 간식을 산다. (He goes home. He buys snacks.)

→ _____

4) 에이미는 졸릴 때까지 공부한다. (Amy studies. Amy feels sleepy.)

→ _____

04 다음 두 문장이 같은 뜻이 되도록 쓰시오.

1) Suzie arrived home when the TV program ended.

= When _____ .

2) Kate played with her friend until it was dark.

= Until _____ .

3) Harry does his homework before he eats dinner.

= After _____ .

4) They went to London after they learned English.

= Before _____ .

05 접속사에 유의하여 다음 문장을 우리말로 해석하시오.

1) The movie started when Suzie arrived at the theater.

→ _____

2) They will go home after they have lunch at a family restaurant.

→ _____

3) Harry will wait until the train arrives.

→ _____

4) Kate drinks water before she has lunch.

→ _____

06 주어진 말을 이용하여 다음 우리말을 영작하시오.

1) 나는 배가 고플 때 바나나를 하나 먹는다. (hungry)

→ _____

2) 그들은 아기가 잠들 때까지 기다렸다. (fall sleep)

→ _____

3) 그들은 방과 후에 축구를 한다.

→ _____

4) 그는 해가 뜨기 전에 일어난다. (rise)

→ _____

Unit 29 ▶ because, if, that

O1 다음 중 알맞은 것을 고르시오.

1) Jane will be sad [if | that] her mom is sick.

2) Harry thinks [because | that] James is an actor.

3) The problem is [if | that] she is weak.

4) Suzie passed the test [because | that] she studied hard.

5) It is impossible [because | that] they become a ballerina.

O2 우리말과 일치하도록 빈칸에 알맞은 말을 쓰시오.

1) 나는 그가 의사라고 생각한다.

　→ I think ＿＿＿＿＿＿＿＿＿ he is a doctor.

2) 만약 비가 온다면 레이는 집에 머무를 것이다.

　→ Ray will stay at home ＿＿＿＿＿＿＿＿ it rains.

3) 제시카는 똑똑하기 때문에 그 문제를 풀 수 있다.

　→ Jessica can solve the problem ＿＿＿＿＿＿＿＿ she is clever.

4) 케이트가 미국 사람이라는 것은 사실이다.

　→ It is true ＿＿＿＿＿＿＿＿ Kate is an American.

O3 두 문장이 같은 뜻이 되도록 만드시오.

1) James worked all day, so he is tired now.

　= Because ＿＿＿＿＿＿＿＿＿＿＿＿＿＿＿＿＿＿＿＿＿＿＿＿.

2) That they lost the game was surprising.

　= It ＿＿＿＿＿＿＿＿＿＿＿＿＿＿＿＿＿＿＿＿＿＿＿＿＿＿.

3) Take an umbrella, and you won't get wet.

　= If ＿＿＿＿＿＿＿＿＿＿＿＿＿＿＿＿＿＿＿＿＿＿＿＿＿＿.

O4 다음 두 문장을 접속사를 사용하여 한 문장으로 만드시오.

1) 그는 키가 컸기 때문에 농구 선수가 되었다. (He was tall. He became a basketball player.)

　→ ＿＿＿＿＿＿＿＿＿＿＿＿＿＿＿＿＿＿＿＿＿＿＿＿＿＿＿

2) 너무 많이 먹는다면 너는 배탈이 날 것이다. (You will have a stomachache. You eat too much.)

　→ ＿＿＿＿＿＿＿＿＿＿＿＿＿＿＿＿＿＿＿＿＿＿＿＿＿＿＿

3) 그녀는 그가 좋은 결정을 했다고 생각한다. (She thinks. He made a good decision.)

　→ ＿＿＿＿＿＿＿＿＿＿＿＿＿＿＿＿＿＿＿＿＿＿＿＿＿＿＿

O5 다음 문장을 우리말로 해석하시오.

1) The answer is that water boils at 100°C.

→ _____

2) I will go to the party if he invites me.

→ _____

3) I hope that she will win the game.

→ _____

4) She walked to school because she missed the bus.

→ _____

5) It is important that everyone in my family is healthy.

→ _____

O6 우리말과 일치하도록 주어진 단어를 알맞게 배열하시오.

1) 나는 그가 기록을 깰 것이라고 믿는다. (believe, will, the, that, break, I, he, record)

→ _____

2) 비가 와서 그는 젖었다. (wet, it, because, he, rained, was)

→ _____

3) 만약 그들이 그것을 한다면 우리는 그들을 도울 것이다. (will, they, if, help, do, them, it, we)

→ _____

4) 아기들이 잠을 많이 자는 것은 자연스럽다. (natural, sleep, that, is, a lot, babies, it)

→ _____

O7 주어진 말을 이용하여 다음 우리말을 영작하시오.

1) 그는 그녀가 고집이 세다고 생각한다. (stubborn)

→ _____

2) 그녀는 피곤하면 쉴 것이다. (take a rest)

→ _____

3) 그가 그녀를 만난다면 그는 그녀와 친구가 될 것이다. (make friends with)

→ _____

4) 그는 아팠기 때문에 일찍 잤다. (go to bed)

→ _____

5) 그가 강하다는 것은 사실이다. (true)

→ _____

01 다음 중 알맞은 전치사를 고르시오.

1) at | on | in Friday   2) at | on | in 1 o'clock

3) at | on | in noon   4) at | on | in November

5) at | on | in December 25   6) at | on | in fall

7) to | on | in weekends   8) at | on | in the evening

9) at | on | in Saturday night 10) at | on | in 2015

02 다음 문장의 빈칸에 at, on, in 중 알맞은 전치사를 쓰시오.

1) The store opens _____ 9:30 _____ the morning.

2) She has 4 classes _____ Wednesday.

3) It rains a lot in Korea _____ summer.

4) He will leave Seoul _____ July 2.

5) We will go on a picnic _____ May.

6) They go to church _____ Sunday mornings.

7) He came back to America _____ 2002.

03 우리말과 일치하도록 빈칸에 알맞은 말을 쓰시오.

1) 그녀는 밤 11시에 잠자리에 든다.

   → She goes to bed _____ eleven o'clock _____ _____.

2) 나의 어머니는 지난주 이후로 계속 바쁘시다.

   → My mother has been busy _____ last week.

3) 그는 여름 방학 동안에 그의 할머니를 방문할 것이다.

   → He will visit his grandmother _____ _____ _____.

4) 나는 2시까지 그를 기다릴 것이다.

   → I will wait for him _____ 2 o'clock.

5) 나의 아버지는 내 생일에 나에게 드레스를 사 주셨다.

   → My father bought a dress for me _____ _____ _____.

6) 나의 가족은 금요일 저녁에 영화를 보았다.

   → My family watched movies _____ _____ _____.

04 전치사와 주어진 표현을 이용하여 다음 질문에 대한 대답을 쓰시오.

1) Ⓐ What time do you go to school?

Ⓑ _____ (half past eight)

2) Ⓐ When does he have drum lessons?

Ⓑ _____ (Friday and Saturday)

3) Ⓐ When did the Korean war break out?

Ⓑ _____ (1950)

4) Ⓐ How long have you known him?

Ⓑ _____ (2010)

05 다음 문장의 틀린 부분에 밑줄을 긋고 바르게 고쳐 쓰시오.

1) 정오에 점심 먹자.

Let's eat lunch in noon.　　　　　　(→ _____)

2) 가을에는 나뭇잎이 빨갛고 노랗게 바뀐다.

Leaves turn red and yellow on autumn.　(→ _____)

3) 그들은 4일 동안 아무것도 먹지 않았다.

They didn't eat anything during four days.　(→ _____)

4) 우리는 밤 10시까지 수학 공부를 했다.

We studied math at 10 o'clock at night.　(→ _____)

5) 나는 1월 17일에 태어났다.

I was born in January 17.　　　　　(→ _____)

06 주어진 말을 이용하여 다음 우리말을 영작하시오.

1) 우리는 5시까지 숙제를 했다.

→ _____

2) 그들은 오후 2시에 아이스크림 가게로 갔다. (ice cream shop)

→ _____

3) 우리는 주말에 일하지 않는다. (on weekends)

→ _____

4) 겨울에는 매우 춥다.

→ _____

5) 그녀는 3시간 동안 도서관에 있었다. (library)

→ _____

O1 다음 중 알맞은 전치사를 고르시오.

1) I usually eat lunch   on | with | in   Sumi.

2) She goes to school   with | on | by   bike.

3) This car is   at | in | for   my father.

4) My house is   in | at | between   the bank and the ice cream shop.

5) There is a clock   in | at | on   the wall.

6) He is leaving   for | on | in   the bus stop.

7) My friend wants to sit   beside | by | next   to me.

8) There is a school   near | next | across   from my house.

9) He went   at | to | with   the post office this morning.

10) There is some bread   on | at | to   the table.

O2 우리말과 일치하도록 빈칸에 알맞은 말을 쓰시오.

1) 우리는 한강을 따라 산책했다.

→ We took a walk _____ the Han River.

2) 몇몇 아이들이 거리를 가로질러 걸어가고 있다.

→ Some children are walking _____ the street.

3) 고양이 한 마리가 상자 안으로 들어 갔다.

→ A cat went _____ the box.

4) 그는 가방 밖으로 몇 권의 만화책을 꺼냈다.

→ He took some comic books _____ _____ his bag.

5) 나의 아버지는 서울에서 부산까지 운전을 했다.

→ My father drove _____ Seoul _____ Busan.

6) 그녀의 양말은 침대 아래에 있다.

→ Her socks are _____ _____ _____ .

7) 한 여자가 교회 앞에 서있다.

→ A lady is standing _____ _____ _____ the church.

8) 너는 나무 뒤에 숨을 수 있다.

→ You can hide _____ the tree.

O3 다음 문장의 <u>틀린</u> 부분에 밑줄을 긋고 바르게 고쳐 쓰시오.

1) 보라는 이층으로 올라갔다.

Bora went down to the second floor. (→ _____)

2) 나의 아버지는 젓가락을 가지고 스파게티를 드신다.

My father eats spaghetti on chopsticks. (→ _____)

3) 나의 할머니댁은 나의 학교 뒤에 있다.

My grandmother's house is in front of my school. (→ _____)

4) 우리는 그를 위해 블로그를 만들었다.

We made a blog for he. (→ _____)

5) 너의 어머니 옆에 있는 소녀는 누구니?

Who is the girl besides your mother? (→ _____)

O4 우리말과 일치하도록 주어진 단어를 알맞게 배열하시오.

1) 그는 주말마다 강을 따라 자전거를 탄다. (rides, he, along, every, a bike, the river, weekend)

→ _____

2) 의자 아래에 새끼 고양이가 두 마리가 있다. (two kittens, there, chair, under, are, the)

→ _____

3) 몇 마리 새들이 나무 위에서 날고 있다. (over, some, flying, birds, are, the tree)

→ _____

4) 나는 숲 속을 걷는 것을 좋아한다. (through, like, walk, I, to, the forest)

→ _____

O5 주어진 말을 이용하여 다음 우리말을 영작하시오.

1) 그녀는 수미(Sumi)와 보라(Bora) 사이에 앉았다.

→ _____

2) 그 서점은 내 친구의 커피숍 앞에 있다. (coffee shop)

→ _____

3) 지호(Jiho)는 우리와 함께 종종 쇼핑을 간다. (go shopping)

→ _____

4) 큰 수박 하나가 오렌지 옆에 있다. (watermelon)

→ _____

5) 그는 화장실 안으로 달려 들어갔다. (toilet)

→ _____